DK EYEWITNESS

T0001132

TOP 10
VENICE

Top 10 Venice Highlights

The Top 10 of Everything

CONTENTS

Venice
Area by Area

Streetsmart

Within each Top 10 list in this book, no hierarchy of quality or popularity is implied. All 10 are, in the editor's opinion, of roughly equal merit.

Title page, front cover and spine *Stunning view of Basilica di Santa Maria della Salute from the docks*
Back cover, clockwise from top left *Tiramisù, a classic Italian dessert; central dome of the Basilica di San Marco; view over Venice rooftops; San Giorgio Maggiore; colourful boats and buildings line a canal*

The rapid rate at which the world is changing is constantly keeping the DK Eyewitness team on our toes. While we've worked hard to ensure that this edition of Venice is accurate and up-to-date, we know that opening hours alter, standards shift, prices fluctuate, places close and new ones pop up in their stead. So, if you notice we've got something wrong or left something out, we want to hear about it. Please get in touch at **travelguides@dk.com**

Welcome to
Venice

Gliding gondolas. Glorious sunsets over the lagoon. Spritz *aperitivos*. Black cuttlefish-ink pasta. Renaissance *palazzi*. Gorgeous Carnival masks. A time warp. And no cars; not one. It doesn't matter how many times you've been, a visit to Venice is as memorable as it is romantic. With DK Eyewitness Top 10 Venice guide, it's yours to explore.

There's nothing like Venice anywhere else in the world. Start in the **Piazza San Marco** and wonder at the architectural splendour of **Basilica di San Marco**. Explore the labyrinthine **Doge's Palace**, take a *vaporetto* ride on the **Grand Cana**l, or travel to the breathtaking islands of **Murano** and **Torcello**. There's also several hundreds of years' worth of art to explore in the **Accademia Galleries** and **Peggy Guggenheim Collection**.

Away from the famous sights, this unique city is just as enchanting. Simply wander its narrow streets, crossing ancient bridges and pausing in *campi* (small squares). Relax at the outdoor cafés, taking in the atmosphere while sipping a cappuccino or a traditional spritz, hunt for a costume for the annual Carnival, and shop at amazing craft stores and fashion boutiques.

Whether you're visiting for a weekend or a week, our Top 10 guide brings together the best of everything that Venice has to offer, from the dazzling art collection of the **Accademia Galleries** to a gondola ride down the meandering **Grand Canal**. The guide has useful tips throughout, including information on free activities and places off the beaten track, plus ten easy-to-follow itineraries, designed to tie together a clutch of sights in a short space of time. Add inspiring photography and detailed maps, and you've got the essential pocket-sized travel companion. **Enjoy the book, and enjoy Venice**.

Clockwise from top: **Giudecca, lion statue in Piazza San Marco, Basilica di San Marco mosaic, Grand Canal, Carnival mask, gondolas with San Giorgio Maggiore in the background, Burano**

Exploring Venice

Venice is a sightseeing paradise for people of all ages. To make the most of a holiday and see the best the city has to offer, here are some time-efficient ideas for both two- and four-day stays.

The Grand Canal cuts a meandering path through Venice and offers a delightful perspective from the water.

Two Days in Venice

Day ❶
MORNING

Start off at the marvellous **Basilica di San Marco** (see pp12–15) before wandering around the **Piazza San Marco** (see pp20–21). The Campanile tower gives a superb view over the city.

AFTERNOON

A visit to the **Doge's Palace** (see pp16–19) can be followed by a laid-back ride on a *vaporetto* all the way up the glorious **Grand Canal** (see pp24–5) past many elegant *palazzi* and under the Accademia and Rialto bridges.

Day ❷
MORNING

Begin with Venetian art at the **Accademia Galleries** (see pp30–31) before strolling through to **Campo Santa Margherita** (see pp38–9) for a bite to eat.

AFTERNOON

It's a short walk to the Venetian Gothic masterpiece **Santa Maria Gloriosa dei Frari** (see pp32–3) and, from there, on to the lovely Campo San Polo square with its great neighbourhood feel.

Four Days in Venice

Day ❶
MORNING

A good place to start any visit is the magnificent main square, **Piazza San Marco** (see pp20–21). Visit the panoramic Campanile or the Torre dell'Orologio (booking essential), then have a coffee at the legendary – but expensive – **Caffè Florian** (see p21). Refreshed, head into the **Basilica di San Marco** (see pp12–15) to wonder at the ancient mosaics.

AFTERNOON

After lunch, take time to explore the **Doge's Palace** (see pp16–19), once the powerhouse of the Maritime Republic. Don't miss the Bridge of Sighs and the dank prisons.

The impressive Doge's Palace dominates the waterfront leading to Piazza San Marco.

The island of Burano is well worth a visit for its splendid array of colourful houses.

Day ❷
MORNING
Catch a *vaporetto* at Piazzale Roma or the railway station for the spectacular trip along the **Grand Canal** (see pp24–5), passing beneath Rialto Bridge. Alight at Salute to visit the **Punta della Dogana** (see p98).
AFTERNOON
After lunch on the sun-blessed **Zattere** (see p97), backtrack to see the impressive **Peggy Guggenheim Collection** (see pp40–41).

Day ❸
MORNING
Make an early start to enjoy the best of **The Rialto** (see pp34–5), a fish and produce market, which is open mostly in the morning. It's then just a short walk to the church of **Santa Maria Gloriosa dei Frari** (see pp32–3), a masterpiece of Venetian Gothic architecture.

AFTERNOON
Campo Santa Margherita (see pp38–9) is a bustling square with inviting cafés and restaurants ideal for lunch. After you have eaten, proceed to the **Accademia Galleries** (see pp30–31) for an overview of Venetian painting through the centuries.

Day ❹
MORNING
Take a leisurely ferry trip over the Northern Lagoon to the island of **Torcello** (see pp36–7), where you can admire the Byzantine mosaics in the Basilica. Then continue to neighbouring **Burano** (see p117) or **Mazzorbo** (see p117) for lunch.
AFTERNOON
Pick up a ferry to take you cruising via Treporti and **Punta Sabbioni** (see p119) to the **Lido** (see pp123–4) for a trip to the beach. Afterwards, head back to Venice proper.

Top 10 Venice Highlights

Basilica di Santa Maria della Salute
viewed from Ponte dell'Accademia

📊 **Venice Highlights**

The uniquely romantic city of Venice was built entirely on water and has managed to survive into the 21st century without cars. Narrow alleyways and canals pass between sumptuous palaces and magnificent churches, colourful neighbourhood markets and quiet backwaters, unchanged for centuries. Few cities possess such an awe-inspiring line-up of sights for visitors.

Basilica di San Marco ①

Venice's fairy-tale cathedral is distinctly Byzantine, and its façade and interior have been embellished with resplendent mosaics and works of art through the ages *(see pp12–15).*

② Doge's Palace

This was the powerhouse of the city's rulers for nearly 900 years. Passing through the maze of gilded rooms gives visitors a fascinating insight into the extravagant lifestyle that so often accompanied state affairs *(see pp16–19).*

③ Piazza San Marco

Elegance and opulence sit side by side in what Napoleon named "the finest drawing room in Europe". This magnificent square is adorned with monuments that bear testimony to Venice's history *(see pp20–23).*

④ Grand Canal

The city's majestic watercourse swarms with all manner of boats, while its embankments has a dazzling succession of palaces dating back as early as the 13th century *(see pp24–7).*

Accademia Galleries

This collection of Venetian paintings includes masterpieces by Titian, Bellini and Giorgione. Not only for art lovers, it is a must for all *(see pp30–31)*.

Santa Maria Gloriosa dei Frari

A Gothic interior with grandiose works of art lies in store behind this church's brick façade *(see pp32–3)*.

The Rialto

Home to the most famous bridge on the Canal Grande, this fresh produce market has enlivened this area since medieval times *(see pp34–5)*.

Torcello

Escape the crowds in the city with a ferry ride over the vast expanse of the lagoon to this peaceful, lush island, the site of Venice's original settlement *(see pp36–7)*.

Campo Santa Margherita

Thanks to its market stalls and outdoor cafés, this lovely square is always bustling with life. An added bonus are the many architectural styles here *(see pp38–9)*.

Peggy Guggenheim Collection

Italy's leading museum for 20th-century European and American art is housed in a palace on the Grand Canal *(see pp40–41)*.

PEGGY GUGGENHEIM COLLECTION

CAMPO SAN STAE

CAMPO DEI SANTI APOSTOLI

PO S. COMO L'ORIO

CAMPO SAN CASSIANO

CAMPO S. GIACOMO DI RIALTO

SAN POLO

CAMPO SAN POLO

RIVA DEL VIN

Ponte di Rialto

Canal Grande

CALLE DEI FABBRI

CAMPO SAN LUCA

CAMPO MANIN

SAN MARCO

CAMPO S. ANGELO

FREZZERIA

MPO SAN AMUELE

CAMPO S. STEFANO

CAMPO S. FANTIN

CPO SAN MOISE

CAMPO S. MAURIZIO

C. LARGA XXII MARZO

CASTELLO

Ponte dell' Accademia

Canal Grande

CAMPO DELLA SALUTE

0 metres 300
0 yards 300

🔟 ⭐ Basilica di San Marco

The breathtaking Byzantine basilica dominating Piazza San Marco was constructed in such ornate fashion for two reasons: as an embodiment of the Venetian Republic's power and as a fitting resting place for St Mark. Serving as the doges' chapel, it was the site of coronations, funerals and processions, all gloriously framed by more than 4,000 sq m (43,000 sq ft) of mosaics, treasures and 500 columns, some dating back to the 3rd century.

Western Façade ①

A marvellous succession of domes, columns, arches and spires **(right)**, interspersed with marble statues, screens and glittering mosaics, greets tourists in Piazza San Marco. The northernmost arch houses 13th-century mosaics that depict the basilica itself. Other mosaics are 17th- and 18th-century copies.

② Atrium Mosaics

These mosaics **(above)** were created in the Byzantine tradition, and give detailed accounts of the Old Testament. The 13th-century cupola's concentric circles recount 24 episodes from Genesis, including the Creation.

③ Flooring

The elaborate paving is a mosaic masterpiece of multicoloured stones on uneven levels, evocative of the sea. Intricate geometrical designs sit alongside animal shapes.

Basilica di San Marco

Pala d'Oro ④

The dazzling jewel-encrusted gold screen **(right)** was commissioned in Constantinople in 976 but frequently added to at later dates. It has 250 panels bearing 1,927 precious stones and gems, and cloisonné plaques.

BUILDING THE BASILICA

Construction first began in 829, but it was burned down in 976, in a revolt. The building dates from 1071. The architect is shown over the central portal, biting his fingers in frustration. The basilica became the city cathedral in 1807.

Ascension Dome 7

The central dome **(right)** has a spectacular array of early 13th-century mosaics, depicting the New Testament. *Christ in Glory* is shown above depictions of the Virtues.

8 Pentecost Dome

What is probably the first dome of the basilica to be adorned with mosaics depicts the Descent of the Holy Ghost, seen as a flame over the heads of the 12 apostles.

9 Basilica Museum

Here you'll find the famed quartet of horses crafted from bronze and covered in gold. Booty from the Fourth Crusade, these restored Graeco-Roman equine figures originally graced the Hippodrome in Constantinople.

Loggia dei Cavalli 10

Replicas of the horses **(right)**, now in the museum, stand on this balcony overlooking Piazza San Marco. Visitors can also see clutches of columns, whose dimensions and decorative styles indicate their origins.

The Tetrarchs 5

The inspiration for these figures **(right)** is unknown. They probably represent the four emperors of the eastern and western Roman empires. The statue was pillaged from Constantinople during the Fourth Crusade in 1204.

6 Treasury

The basilica's glittering riches include precious chalices of rock crystal enamelled by medieval silver- and goldsmiths and reliquaries from Venice's eastern conquests, including parts of the True Cross.

NEED TO KNOW

MAP Q5 ■ Piazza San Marco ■ 041 270 83 11 ■ www.basilicasanmarco.it

Guided visits: book on www.alata.it

Basilica: Open 9:30am–5:15pm Mon-Sat (from 2pm Sun & hols; last admission 4:45pm); adm 3€

Pala d'Oro, treasury and Loggia dei Cavalli: 9:30am–5:15pm Mon-Sat (from 2pm Sun & hols; last admission 4:45pm); adm Pala d'Oro €5; treasury €7

Museum: Open 9:45am–5:45pm daily (last admission 4:45pm); adm €7

■ Pre-book tickets online to beat the queues.

■ Visit at dusk, when the setting sun lights up the façade.

■ Take binoculars to examine the mosaics, but you must leave backpacks in the luggage room.

Basilica Architectural Features

1 Galleries
The airy catwalks over the body of the basilica reflect the eastern tradition of segregation in worship, as they were exclusively for women. They are closed to visitors.

2 Stone Wall-Slabs
Brick-faced until the 1100s, the walls of the basilica were then covered with stone slabs from the East, sliced lengthways to produce a kaleidoscopic effect.

3 Romanesque Stone Carvings
The exquisite semicircular stone carvings over the central doorway were executed between 1235 and 1265 and still bear traces of their original colouring.

4 The "Victory Bringer"
This revered Byzantine icon is given pride of place in the Madonna of Nicopeia Chapel. Rumoured to have been executed by St Luke, it was carried into battle for its miraculous powers.

5 Baptistry
Aglow with 14th-century mosaic scenes of the life of St John, this is also home to the tomb of Italian architect Jacopo Sansovino (see p55). Open for prayer only.

Basilica di San Marco

6 Zen Chapel
The ornate decoration in this chapel was executed for the funeral of its namesake, Cardinal Zen, in 1521, in recognition of his gifts to the state. Open for prayer only.

The ornate Iconostasis

7 Iconostasis
This elaborate screen separates the worship area of the chancel from the nave. Atop its eight columns are Gothic-style statues of the Virgin and the apostles, sculpted by the Dalle Masegne brothers in 1394.

8 Byzantine Pierced Screens
Influenced by eastern architecture, delicate geometrical designs and lattice-work stone screens are featured on all three façades, in the atrium and loggia.

9 Porta dei Fiori
This doorway on the northern façade bears a 13th-century nativity scene surrounded by Moorish arches.

10 Altar Columns
Four finely carved alabaster and marble columns support a canopy at the altar, beneath which lies the body of St Mark.

Font in the Baptistry

ST MARK, PATRON SAINT OF VENICE

Although the well-loved saint of Byzantium St Theodore had been appointed protector of Venice by the Byzantine emperor, the fledgling republic felt in need of a saint of its own. According to legend, in 828 CE, two adroit Venetian merchants filched the body of St Mark from a monastery in Alexandria, transporting it under layers of pork fat to conceal it from Muslim guards. The welcome in Venice was triumphant, and the story was recounted in countless paintings and mosaics. The remains, however, were mislaid for years, until an arm miraculously broke through a column in 1094 (marked by a small cross, left of the Altar of the Sacrament) in answer to a prayer. St Mark now rests in peace beneath the basilica's main altar. The ubiquitous winged lion representing St Mark could be found throughout the republic as the trademark of Venetian dominion: it is often

shown with two paws in the sea and two on land, to symbolize the geography of Venice.

TOP 10
VENICE RELICS

1 Milk of the Virgin Mary, Basilica Treasury *(see p13)*

2 Blood of Christ, Basilica Treasury

3 Nail from the True Cross, Chiesa di San Pantalon *(see p49)*

4 Thorn from Christ's crown, Basilica Treasury

5 Body of St Mark, Basilica di San Marco *(see pp12–13)*

6 Body of St Lucy, Chiesa di San Geremia

7 Three rocks used to stone St Stephen to death, Basilica Treasury

8 Skull of St John the Baptist, Basilica Treasury

9 Leg of St George, Basilica Treasury

10 Foot of St Catherine of Siena, Santi Giovanni e Paolo *(see p48)*

The Miracle of the Relic of the True Cross on the Rialto Bridge **(1494) by Vittore Carpaccio**

This mosaic in Basilica San Marco depicts the veneration of the body of St Mark by the Doge.

🔟 ⭐ **Doge's Palace**

A magnificent combination of Byzantine, Gothic and Renaissance architecture, the Palazzo Ducale (Doge's Palace) was the official residence of the 120 doges who ruled Venice from 697 to 1797. A fortress-like structure stood here in the 9th century, to be replaced by the elegant Gothic version seen today, despite a string of fires in the 1500s. Artists such as Titian, Tintoretto and Bellini vied with each other to embellish the palace with painting and sculpture, not to mention architects Antonio Rizzo and Pietro Lombardo, the latter responsible for the western façade.

1 Façade

Elegant twin façades **(above)** face the piazzetta and the quayside. Pink-and-cream stonework and a loggia stand above an arcade of columns with 36 sculpted Istrian stone capitals.

2 Sala del Senato

Senate members met in this lavish hall **(below)** to debate war, foreign affairs and trade with the Doge. Time was measured by two clocks – one with a 24-hour face, the other with zodiac signs.

3 Armoury

This is a gripping, if spine-chilling, collection of beautifully crafted firearms, ceremonial weapons and suits of armour **(left)** from Asia and the West. Among the war trophies is a Turkish standard brought back from the Battle of Lepanto (1571).

4 Prisons

A fascinating maze of cells is linked by corridors and staircases on both sides of the canal. One of the most famous inmates, Casanova *(see p50)*, made a dramatic escape across the roof in 1756. The "new prisons" were in use until the 1940s and feature poignant graffiti by internees.

THE GREAT COUNCIL
By the mid-16th century the Great Council had around 2,000 members. Any Venetian of high birth over 25 years old was entitled to a seat – with the exception of those married to a commoner. From 1646, merchants could purchase a seat with 100,000 ducats.

Scala d'Oro ⑦
The magnificent Golden Staircase (right), so-called for its Classical stucco decorations in 24-carat gold-leaf framing frescoes, led guests of honour to the second floor. Designed by Sansovino (see p55), it was later completed by Scarpagnino in 1559.

⑤ Bridge of Sighs
One of the world's most famous bridges (above), the Ponte dei Sospiri is an early 17th-century Baroque structure that crosses to the palace prisons. It reputedly caused the condemned to "sigh" at their last glimpse of sky and sea.

⑥ Sala dello Scudo
Enormous globes (below) and painted wall maps showing the known world in 1762 make this room a must. The map of Eastern Asia traces Marco Polo's travels to China, complete with camels, rhinos and the mythical Uncharted Lands of the People Eaters.

⑧ Sala del Maggior Consiglio
The Great Council Chamber is lined with canvases of Venetian victories and a cornice frieze of 76 doges – a black curtain represents traitor Marin Falier (see p19).

⑩ Porta della Carta
The palace's main entrance (left), which is now the visitors' exit, has a beautifully sculpted 1438 portal by the Bon family. The name "paper door" arose because edicts were posted here.

⑨ Doge's Apartments
The communicating rooms of the Doge's living quarters include rich brocades, triumphal friezes, gilded ceilings and works of art.

NEED TO KNOW
MAP R5
■ Piazza San Marco
■ 041 427 308 92
■ www.visitmuve.it

Open 9am–6pm (last admission 5pm); 6 Jan, 9, 10, 23 Dec: 9am–9pm; 1 Jan & 25 Dec: 10am–6pm (last admission 5pm)

Adm €25 online in advance/€30 (includes entry to the Museo Correr Complex; €13 online in advance/€15 concessions)

Secret Itineraries Tour: 848 08 20 00 (advance booking essential, online or by phone); 10am, 11:30am & 1pm daily in English; tickets: €32 (€20 concessions)

■ The Secret Itineraries Tour through hidden chambers of the palace is highly recommended.

■ The Museo dell' Opera, near the ticket office, houses many of the original 14th-century façade capitals – those outside are mostly 19th-century copies.

Doge's Palace Art and Architecture

Veronese's *Rape of Europa*

1 Rape of Europa
Veronese's allegorical work (1580) in the Anti-Collegio shows Europa sitting on a bull, alias Jove, who is nuzzling her foot.

2 Paradise
Possibly the world's largest oil painting (1588–90), *Paradise* by Jacopo and Domenico Tintoretto is said to contain 800 figures (Sala del Maggior Consiglio).

3 Arcade Capital
Proclaimed the "most beautiful in Europe" by art critic John Ruskin, this eight-sided carved capital on the southwest corner shows the zodiac signs and planets in imaginative detail.

4 The Triumph of Venice
Dominating the Sala del Senato is Tintoretto's glorious work of propaganda (1580–84), showing allegorical and mytho-logical figures proffering fruits of the sea to Venice.

5 Central Balcony
This magnificent early 15th-century stone terrace, embellished with columns, spires and a host of saints, opens off the Sala del Maggior Consiglio with a breathtaking view of the lagoon.

6 Arco Foscari
This triumphal archway of pink-and-cream stone layers leading to the Giants' Staircase was commissioned by Doge Foscari in 1438.

7 Wellheads
Elaborate 16th-century well-heads were constructed to drain water from the gutters to the palace's central courtyard.

8 Drunkenness of Noah
A powerful sculpture from the early 15th century adorns the façade's southeast corner. Noah, inebriated and half-naked before his sons, is intended to portray the weakness of man.

Drunkenness of Noah

9 Coronation of the Virgin
The faded but inspired remains of Guariento's fresco, discovered beneath Tintoretto's *Paradise*, are housed in a side room, with panels explaining the restoration techniques.

10 Giants' Staircase
So named for its two colossal statues of Mars and Neptune, which were sculpted by Sansovino in 1567 as symbols of Venice's power. Visiting dignitaries would ascend the marble-lined stairs to the palace.

Giants' staircase, Doge's Palace

THE EXTENT OF THE VENETIAN REPUBLIC

Doge Gradenigo with the Venetian fleet at the siege of Chioggia, 1379

In its earliest days, Venice was little more than a huddle of islands in the middle of a shallow marshy lagoon, settled by a band of refugees from the Veneto region. Yet over the centuries it developed into a mighty republic reaching south to the Mediterranean and north to the Alps, based on the concept of trade. Salt was stored in massive warehouses, there were dealings in spices and wondrous fabrics from the East, crusades were organized and fitted out here, and relics procured. Its main population probably never exceeded 160,000, however, well beyond its walled port towns, which stretched down the Dalmatian coast, were far-flung outposts such as Crete and Cyprus. These dominions protected key passages in commerce with the Arabic countries. Westward across the Po plain, Venice's influence took in Treviso, Vicenza and Verona, extending all the way to Bergamo on the outskirts of Milan and the mighty Visconti dynasty.

The Republic's gaining of maritime power is celebrated in *The Victorious Return of Doge Andrea Contarini after Triumph in Chioggia* by Paolo Veronese (1525–88).

TOP 10
EVENTS IN THE VENETIAN REPUBLIC

1 Venice founded on 25 April (St Mark's Day, 421 CE)

2 First doge, Paoluccio Anafesto, elected (697)

3 St Mark's body brought to Venice (828)

4 Ruthless siege of Constantinople during the Fourth Crusade under Doge Enrico Dandolo (1204)

5 Venice loses 60 per cent of its population to the Black Death (1348)

6 Doge Marin Falier decapitated for conspiracy (1355)

7 Genoese defeated at Battle of Chioggia, leaving Venice to reign over the Adriatic and Mediterranean (1381)

8 Victory over Turks at Battle of Lepanto (1571)

9 After 25 years of war, Crete is lost to the Turks (1669)

10 Napoleon invades the Veneto, bringing about the fall of the Venetian Republic (1797)

★ Piazza San Marco

Long the political and religious heart of Venice, it's hard to believe Piazza San Marco was once just a monastery garden crossed by a stream. The glittering basilica and Doge's Palace command the east side of the square, while other stately buildings along its borders have been the backdrop for magnificent processions. The western end was remodelled by Napoleon, who wished to construct a royal palace here. Today the piazza continues to bustle, with a museum complex, cafés and costumed Carnival crowds.

1 **Basilica di San Marco**
See pp12–15.

2 **Doge's Palace**
See pp16–19.

3 **Torre dell'Orologio**

This Renaissance-style clock tower is topped by two bronze Moors **(left)** hammering out the hours on the upper terrace. At Epiphany and Ascension there is an hourly procession of clockwork Magi that are led by an angel. According to legend, the crafters were subsequently blinded to prevent them repeating the work.

The Piazzetta and the Palace

NEED TO KNOW

MAP Q5

Campanile: Open 9:30am–9:15pm daily (last admission 8:45pm); closed in certain weather; book guided tours on www.venetoinside.com; adm €10

Torre dell'Orologio: 041 427 308 92 (from abroad); 848 082 000 (from Italy); guided tours: times vary, check website; adm €14 (€11 concessions); book online on www.muve.vivaticket.it

Museo Correr Complex: Open 10am–5pm (last admission 60 mins before closing time); adm €30 (includes Doge's Palace); €15 concessions

Caffè Florian: 041 520 5641; open 9:30am–9pm Mon–Thu, 9am–9pm Sun & 9am–11pm Fri & Sat

Campanile **4**
Incomparable views of the city and lagoon can be had by taking the elevator to the top of this 98-m (323-ft) bell tower **(right)**. It was masterfully rebuilt to its 16th-century design following its clamorous collapse in 1902.

5 **Piazzetta**
Once an inlet for boats and witness to the arrival of distinguished visitors during the Republic's heyday, this now fully paved mini square fronts the lagoon.

7 Column of San Marco

This is one of two granite columns (left) erected in 1172 by Nicolò Barattieri; the other symbolizes San Teodoro. Public executions were held here.

Piazza San Marco

VENICE'S BELLS

Booming through the city, the five bells in the Campanile have been employed to mark Venice's rhythms for centuries. The Maleficio bell was sounded to announce an execution, the Nona rang at midday, the Trottiera spurred on the nobles' horses for assemblies in the Doge's Palace and the Mezza Terza was used to indicate that the Senate was in session. The Marangona bell is still sounded to mark midnight.

6 Procuratie Vecchie and Nuove

The Procurators, who were responsible for state administration, lived in these elegant 15th-century buildings (below).

8 Piazzetta dei Leoncini

This is the site of a former vegetable market, where a pair of small lions (leoncini) carved from red Verona stone (right) have been crouching since 1722.

9 Caffè Florian

Reputedly Europe's first coffee house (see p83), the premises still retain their original 1720 wood-panelling, marble-topped tables and gilt-framed mirrors.

10 Giardinetti Reali

These shady public gardens, created during the Napoleonic era, took the place of boatyards and grain stores, situated just behind the panoramic waterfront.

Museo Correr Complex

1 Biblioteca Marciana Ceiling
The ceiling vault of the opulent reading room (*sale monumentali*), inside the Libreria Sansoviniana, collapsed in 1545 and architect Sansovino imprisoned – he was released to complete the job at his own expense. Titian selected artists for the decorations; Veronese was awarded a gold chain for the best work.

2 Libreria Sansoviniana Staircase
Bedecked with gilt and stucco decorations by Alessandro Vittoria, the 16th-century staircase leads from a monumental entrance on the piazza to the halls of the old library.

Canova's statue of Orpheus

3 Veneziano Paintings
This prolific Byzantine artist is featured in the Pinacoteca's Room 25 (part of Museo Correr), with glowing two-dimensional religious portraits (1290–1302).

Tasteful Correr Ballroom

4 Correr Ballroom
This showy Neo-Classical creation was built for Napoleon. It is now used for exhibitions.

5 Two Venetian Ladies
Carpaccio's masterpiece of well-dressed ladies (1500–10) is in Room 38 of the Museo Correr. It was first thought to depict courtesans because of the ladies' décolléte dresses, but the women are, in fact, awaiting their menfolk's return from hunting.

6 Canova Statues
In the Museo Correr, works by Antonio Canova (1767–1822), foremost sculptor of his time, include his acclaimed statues of Orpheus and Eurydice.

7 Map of Venice
The place of pride in Room 32 of the Museo Correr goes to Jacopo de' Barbari's prospective map-layout of Venice (1497–1500), which was painstakingly engraved on six pear-wood panels.

8 Bellini Room
Works by the talented Bellini family are on display in Room 36 of the Pinacoteca: the poignant *Dead Christ Supported by Two Angels* (1453–5) by the best known, Giovanni; head of the family Jacopo's *Crucifixion* (1450); and son Gentile's portrait of *Doge Giovanni Mocenigo* (1475).

9 Narwhal Tusk
Once prized as the horn of the fabled unicorn, this 1.6-m- (5-ft-) long tusk from the rare whale has been superbly carved with Jesse's and Jesus's family tree (Room 40 in Museo Correr).

10 Crafts and Guilds
Wooden sandals 60-cm (24-inches) high, inlaid with mother-of-pearl, illustrate the stiff demands put upon followers of 15th- to 17th-century fashion (Room 48).

ACQUA ALTA FLOODING

Acqua Alta ("high water") has long been disruptive to the city between October and March, however, it has also become unpredictable with time. As warning sirens fill the air, people drag out their waterproof boots, shopkeepers rush to put up barriers and street-sweepers lay out duck-boards in low-lying spots. Venice and its lagoon are subject to the tides of the Adriatic Sea but flood levels are caused by the coincidence of low atmospheric pressure, strong sirocco winds from the south and natural high tides due to moon phases. Piazza San Marco is one of the most vulnerable spots. The flood gates designed for the Lido sea entrances are held by many experts to be both useless and harmful to the lagoon. However, there are plans for a drainage system on the piazza, dredging canals and raising paving levels.

Bullfight in St Mark's Square by Canaletto and Giovanni Battista Cimaroli

TOP 10
HISTORIC EVENTS IN PIAZZA SAN MARCO

1 Foundations of Doge's Palace laid (814 CE)

2 Construction of basilica started (828)

3 Square paved with brick, herring-bone-style (1267)

4 Square paved with volcanic trachyte blocks (1722–35)

5 Napoleon demolishes San Geminiano church to make way for Ala Napoleonica (1810)

6 Campanile crumbles to the ground (1902)

7 Record flood 1.94 m (6.4 ft) above sea level (4 November 1966)

8 Pink Floyd rock concert attracts 100,000 (1989)

9 Campanile stormed by Venetian separatists (1997)

10 Flood 1.87 m (6.1 ft) above sea level (2019)

Piazza San Marco is located in a vulnerable position on the edge of the lagoon and has been flooded by high tides throughout its history.

TOP 10 ⭐ **Grand Canal**

Venice's majestic "highway", the Canal Grande, is only one of the 177 canals flowing through the city, but at some 4 km (2.5 miles) in length, 30–70 m (98–230 ft) in width and averaging 4.5 m (15 ft) in depth, it certainly earns its name. Snaking its way through the city with a double curve, its banks are lined with exquisite palaces, while on its waters colourful flotillas of gondolas, ferries, taxi launches, high-speed police boats and barges groaning under fresh produce provide endless fascination. In 1818, when the water was cleaner, Lord Byron swam all the way down the Grand Canal from the Lido.

1 Fondaco dei Turchi

With an ornate air and its round arches, this Veneto-Byzantine building **(above)**, dating from 1225, was the Turkish trade centre for 200 years. It is now the Natural History Museum *(see p62)*.

2 Ca' Pesaro

This colossal Baroque palace *(see p57)*, decorated with diamond-point ashlar work, was the final creation of architect Longhena. Home to the city's modern art collections, it is beautifully floodlit at night.

The view towards Santa Maria della Salute

3 Rialto Bridge

One of the city's most familiar sights, the striking 28-m- (92-ft-) wide, 8-m- (26-ft-) high Istrian stone Ponte di Rialto **(below)** dates from 1588.

4 Riva del Vin

A sunny quayside with a string of open-air restaurants, this is one of the few accessible banks of the Grand Canal. Barrels of wine *(vino)* used to be off-loaded here, hence the name.

5 Ca' Rezzonico

The finest feature of this imposing palace is its grandiose staircase **(right)**. Today it is a museum of 18th-century Venice.

6 Accademia Bridge
The lovely wooden Ponte dell'Accademia **(above)**, built in 1932 by the engineer Miozzi, was intended as a temporary measure until a more substantial structure was designed, but it is now a permanent fixture. It affords stunning views of the Grand Canal.

7 Ca' Dario
With an ornamental Renaissance façade studded with multicoloured stone medallions, this lopsided palace is supposedly cursed due to a number of misfortunes that have overtaken its various owners.

8 Santa Maria della Salute
Longhena's 17th-century masterpiece of sculpted whorls beneath a towering dome **(right)**, this church *(see p48)* commemorates the end of a devastating plague in the city.

WAVE DAMAGE

Damage to buildings caused by wash has worsened of late with the rise in motor-propelled craft. Waves provoked by all boats eat into foundations of buildings on the water's edge, as well as making life harder for the gondoliers. Speed limits aim to curb this: 7 kmph (4.5 mph) for private craft and 11 kmph (7 mph) for waterbuses on the Grand Canal. Narrower canals mean 5 kmph (3 mph), while 20 kmph (12.5 mph) is the lagoon maximum.

NEED TO KNOW

The Grand Canal runs from Piazzale Roma, the bus terminal and car park area, to Piazza San Marco. It is easily navigable courtesy of ferries Nos. 1 (all stops) and 2 (main stops only)

■ Take the *vaporetto* line No. 1 to enjoy the best views of the sights along the canal.

■ To beat the crowds, start out from Piazzale Roma heading towards San Marco in the late afternoon or evening, or take the reverse direction in the morning.

9 Punta della Dogana
The figure of Fortune **(right)** stands atop the erstwhile customs house, now an arts centre *(see p98)*, and doubles as a weather vane. This is where the Grand Canal joins St Mark's Basin.

10 Harry's Bar
The legendary watering hole *(see p71)* of Ernest Hemingway is where the Bellini *aperitivo* was invented. Opened in 1931 by Arrigo Cipriani, it was named after the American who funded it.

Watercraft of Venice

Typical Venetian gondola

1 Gondola

These are most often seen transporting tourists around the canals. A larger version *(traghetto)* is also used for the cross-canal ferry *(see p139)*, while the smaller *gondolino* is a slender racing craft.

2 Vaporetto

Strictly speaking, this is the capacious rounded waterbus, now also seen in an "ecological" electric model. A slimmer *motoscafo* serves the outer runs and narrow canals with relatively low bridges.

3 Sandolo

A slim, lightweight boat perfectly suited to hunting and fishing in the shallow waters of the lagoon, not to mention racing. Painted black, these "imitation gondolas" can deceive tourists on the back canals.

4 Topo

The most common barge for transporting goods around the canals, the *topo* can be seen loaded with everything from washing machines to demijohns, often with a live dog "figurehead" on the prow.

5 Sanpierota

This flat-bottomed rowing boat is named after the inhabitants of San Pietro in Volta *(see p125)* in the southern lagoon. Once used for transporting fish to Venice, nowadays it is fitted with an outboard motor and photogenic oblique sail.

6 Bragozzo

With its gently rounded prow and stern, this brightly coloured sailing boat was traditionally used for fishing by the inhabitants of Chioggia *(see p125)*.

7 Fire Boat

From their station near Ca' Foscari, the red launches are called both to deal with fires and to rescue submerged obstacles and crumbling façades.

8 Garbage Vessel

The city's hefty waste-collecting AMAV barges trundle over the lagoon with the day's rubbish, in addition to carrying out environmental monitoring.

Ambulance launch

9 Ambulance and Police Launches

These modern craft attract plenty of attention as they roar down the canals – only the emergency categories are allowed to disregard the city's speed limits.

10 Car Ferry

These giants convey all manner of motor vehicles from the Tronchetto to the Lido.

VENICE'S GONDOLAS

The quintessential sleek Venetian gondola has been plying the city's canals since as early as the 11th century, although it did not take on its present graceful form until the late 1400s. Compared to a mere 405 gondolas on the waterways today, as many as 10,000 were in use in the late 19th century: bridges were once few and far between and gondolas acted as ferries between one island and another, a custom that continues to this day across the Grand Canal by the *traghetti*. A handful of gondola yards still construct the boats as well as carry out repairs, such as San Trovaso in Dorsoduro *(see p98)*. It's a costly and complex craft – eight different types of wood are needed for a total of 280 pieces to make the asymmetrical craft, 11 m (36 ft) in length and 1.42 m (4.5 ft) in width, at a cost approaching €25,000.

**TOP 10
GONDOLA FEATURES**

1 *Forcola* (rowlock)

2 *Ferro* (prow bracket)

3 *Hippocampus* (side ornament)

4 Night lamp

5 Bronze stern decoration

6 Ribbed oar

7 *Felze* (cabin)

8 Gondolier's foot rest

9 Gondolier's striped shirt

10 Gondolier's straw hat

The iron bracket (ferro) on the prow weighs 30 kg (66 lb) to offset the weight of the rower, and adds to the more than 350-kg (770-lb) weight of the gondola. Originally painted in bright colours, the black gondolas that you see today were decreed by the Senate to prevent excessive shows of wealth.

Gondola repair yard

TOP 10 ⭐ Accademia Galleries

A great collection of masterpieces spanning the full development of Venetian art from Byzantine to Renaissance, Baroque and Rococo, the Gallerie dell'Accademia is Venice's equivalent of the Uffizi in Florence. Giovanni Battista Piazzetta started the collection in 1750 to serve as models for the art school; in 1807 it was boosted by Napoleon with the addition of works from suppressed churches. The same year the collection moved to its present premises, occupying three former religious establishments: the 12th–15th-century Scuola Grande di Santa Maria della Carità and its adjoining church, and a 12th-century monastery remodelled by Palladio in the 1500s. In the 1940s, architect Carlo Scarpa modernized the interior spaces.

San Giobbe Altarpiece ❶
Giovanni Bellini's inspirational altarpiece **(right)** (Room II) was painted in 1487 for the Church of San Giobbe. It is regarded as one of the finest examples of Sacra Conversazione, which was central to 15th-century Venetian art. The presence of St Sebastian and St Giobbe beside the Virgin suggests the aftermath of plague, while angel musicians pay homage to San Giobbe, patron saint of music.

❷ The Tempest
This enigmatic 1506 portrayal of a woman suckling her child **(left)** is

by Giorgione (Room VIII). The overall impression is of the figures and the dream-like, stormy landscape blended into one whole.

❸ Supper in the House of Levi
The forceful canvas by Veronese (1573) occupies an entire wall and caused controversy in its time (Room X). The church authorities, who commissioned it as "The Last Supper", were angered by the inclusion of "dogs, buffoons, drunken Germans, dwarfs and other such absurdities" – so Veronese changed the title.

❹ Pietà
Titian's last work (1576) is unfinished but it is also considered his best (Room XI). The Pietà is imbued with golden light and a piercing sense of anguish.

Previous pages Gondolas on the Grand Canal

⑤ Meeting and Departure of the Betrothed Ursula and Ereo

Part of Carpaccio's magnificent narrative cycle (1495) about a Breton princess and an English prince can be seen in Room XXI.

Accademia Galleries

⑥ Procession in St Mark's Square

Part of Gentile Bellini's spectacular cycle (1496) of the St Mark's Day procession in 1444 **(above)** can be seen in Room XX.

⑦ Madonna dell'Arancio

This exquisite work (1496–8) by Cima da Conegliano, painted for a Murano Franciscan church, is enlivened with partridges and plant life (Room II).

NEED TO KNOW

MAP L6 ■ Campo della Carità, Dorsoduro 1050 ■ 041 520 03 45 ■ www.gallerieaccademia.it

Open 8:15am–7:15pm daily (to 2pm Mon; last admission an hour before closing time); closed 1 Jan, 1 May, 25 Dec

Adm €12, €2 youth (18–25) and concessions; free every first Sun of the month

■ The galleries are currently undergoing extensive expansion, so the floorplan may differ from that shown here until completed.

Gallery Guide

The vast gallery is organized in chronological order for the most part and the rooms, labelled with roman numerals, have explanatory cards in English. The Quadreria corridor is filled with masterpieces.

⑧ Coronation of the Virgin

This resplendent polyptych (1350) by Venice's leading 14th-century artist, Paolo Veneziano, is the first work in Room I. Flanking the stunning Byzantine-inspired central piece are events depicted from the life of Christ.

⑨ Portrait of a Gentleman

Lorenzo Lotto's sombre image **(above)** of a melancholic man of means in his study (1528) may be a self-portrait (Room IX). Lotto was known for works of psychological insight.

⑩ Lion of St Mark with Saints John the Baptist, John the Evangelist, Mary Magdalene and Jerome

This marvellous canvas by Cima di Conegliano depicts a winged lion flanked by four saints (Room VIb).

🔟 ⭐ Santa Maria Gloriosa dei Frari

A masterpiece of Venetian Gothic ecclesiastical architecture, this cavernous 15th-century church for Franciscan friars took more than 100 years to complete, along with its "brother" SS Giovanni e Paolo, and a further 26 years for the consecration of the main altar. A wonderful series of art treasures is held within the deceptively gloomy interior, which is almost 100-m (330-ft) long and 50-m (165-ft) across, from priceless canvases by Titian and Bellini to tombs of doges and artists such as Canova.

4 Assumption of the Virgin

Titian's glowing 1518 depiction **(left)** of the triumphant ascent of Mary shows her robed in crimson accompanied by a semicircle of saints, while the 12 apostles are left gesticulating in wonderment below. This brilliant canvas on the high altar is the inevitable focus of the church.

Santa Maria Gloriosa dei Frari

1 Rood Screen

This beautiful screen **(right)**, which divides the worship area and nave is carved in a blend of Renaissance and Gothic styles by Pietro Lombardo and Bartolomeo Bon (1475). It is also decorated with marble figures.

5 Campanile

The robust 14th-century bell tower set into the church's left transept is the second tallest in Venice.

2 Choir Stalls

Unique for Venice, the original three tiers of 124 friars' seats deserve close examination for their inlaid woodwork. Crafted by Marco Cozzi in 1468, they demonstrate the influence of northern European styles.

3 Madonna Enthroned with Saints

Tucked away in the sacristy, and still in its original engraved frame, is another delight for Bellini fans (1488). "It seems painted with molten gems," wrote Henry James of the triptych.

STATE ARCHIVES

The labyrinthine monastery and courtyards adjoining the church have been home to Venice's State Archives since the fall of the Republic. Its 300 rooms and approximately 70 km (43 miles) of shelves are loaded with precious records documenting the history of Venice right back to the 9th century, including the Golden Book register of the Venetian aristocracy. Scholars enter the building via the Oratorio di San Nicolò della Lattuga (1332), named after the miraculous recovery of a Procurator of San Marco thanks to the healing qualities of a lettuce (*lattuga*).

Canova's Mausoleum 6

This colossal monument (right), based on Canova's Neo-Classical design for Titian's tomb, which was never built, was a tribute by the sculptor's followers in 1822.

Monument to Doge Francesco Foscari 8

This is a fine Renaissance tribute to the man responsible for Venice's mainland expansion. Foscari was the subject of Lord Byron's *The Two Foscari*, which was turned into an opera by Verdi.

Statue of John the Baptist 9

The inspirational wood statue (right) of John the Baptist from 1450, which was created especially for the church by artist Donatello (1386–1466), stands in the Florentine chapel. The striking emaciated carved figure is renowned for being particularly lifelike.

Monument to Titian 10

Titian was afforded special authorization for burial here after his death during the 1576 plague, although this sturdy mausoleum was not built for another 300 years.

Santa Maria Gloriosa dei Frari

Mausoleum of Doge Giovanni Pesaro 7

The monsters and black marble figures supporting the sarcophagus of this macabre Baroque monument prompted art critic John Ruskin to write "it seems impossible for false taste and base feeling to sink lower".

NEED TO KNOW

MAP L3 ■ Campo dei Frari, San Polo ■ 041 272 86 11 ■ www.chorus venezia.org or www.basilicadeifrari.it

Open 9am–6pm Mon–Sat, 1–6pm Sun (last admission 30 min before closing time); closed 1 Jan, Easter, 15 Aug, 25 Dec

Adm €5, €2 (12–29 years old), €3 (over 65s); chorus pass €12 (includes admission to 15 churches)

■ Campo dei Frari has some great cafés.

■ Enjoy the nativity scene with lighting effects and moving figures at Christmas.

🔟⭐ **The Rialto**

The commercial hub of Venice, centred on the Rialto Bridge, is as bustling today as it has always been – records tell of markets here since 1097. The area is also the city's historical heart and took its name from Rivoaltus, the high consolidated terrain that guaranteed early settlers flood-free premises. Most buildings, however, date from the 16th century, because a fire swept through Rialto in 1514. During Carnival the stall-holders don medieval costume to vie with each other for custom and only the new awnings and electronic cash registers hint at the modern world.

① Fresh Produce Market

The market here is a treat for the senses, with artistic piles of luscious peaches and cherries, thorny artichokes and red chicory from Treviso. Fruit, vegetables (**above**) and fish are strictly seasonal.

Rialto market alongside the Grand Canal

③ San Giacomo di Rialto

The oldest church in Venice claims to have a foundation set by a pious carpenter in the 5th century, although the present building is medieval. The Gothic portico and 24-hour clock are well worth a look.

④ Public Rostrum

New laws and names of criminals were announced atop this porphyry column (**right**), supported by a stone figure known as *il gobbo* (hunchback).

② Pescheria

Writhing eels, huge swordfish, soft-shelled crabs and crimson-fleshed fresh tuna are among the stars of the 1907 Neo-Gothic fish market hall (**above**), barely out of reach of the scavenging seagulls.

⑤ Palazzo dei Camerlenghi

This lopsided 1525 palace once imprisoned debtors on the ground floor, while the top floors served as offices for the city *camerlenghi* (treasurers).

6 Gondola Ferry
A must for every visitor is a trip on the *traghetto* ferry **(left)** across the Grand Canal – one of only eight still in operation. Custom dictates that passengers should remain standing.

7 Banco Giro Arcade
Merchants from the East and the West gathered to exchange a variety of goods, including silks and spices, outside the city's first bank set up in 1157, which is now a wine bar.

PLACE NAMES

Rialto market's narrow alleyways carry names such as Orefici (goldsmiths), Pescaria (fishmongers) and Erberia (vegetables), because the same type of shops once stood together. Local eateries for market traders also had evocative names such as Scimia (Monkey) and Do Mori (Two Moors).

8 Ruga degli Orefici
This lovely covered passageway decorated with frescoes has been home to silversmiths, goldsmiths and silk traders since the 1300s.

9 Fabbriche Nuove
Uniformed *carabinieri* (police) patrol the elongated law courts along the Grand Canal. Designed in 1552–5 by Sansovino they are recognizable by their 25 plain arcades.

10 Grand Canal Views
The Erberia, right on the Grand Canal **(below)**, makes a wonderful spot for boat-watching. Alternatively, wander on to the Rialto Bridge for a different vantage point.

NEED TO KNOW

MAP P2 ■ San Polo ■ Fresh produce market: 7:30am–8pm Mon–Sat; Pescheria: 7:30am–2pm Tue–Sat

■ In addition to fresh fruit from the market, picnic supplies can be bought at the delicatessens and bakeries in the neighbourhood.

⭐ Torcello

Reached by a beautiful 60-minute ferry ride from northern Venice, the laid-back island of Torcello is home to the lagoon's oldest building – the basilica – and has an intriguing history. From the 5th century, mainlanders fleeing invading Lombards and Huns ventured across tidal flats to found a settlement here that grew to 20,000 and lasted 1,000 years. However, few clues to the past remain, as the canals silted up, malaria decimated the population and the power base shifted to Venice once and for all. Today, Torcello is home to a handful of gardeners and fishers.

Torcello Basilica Exterior ①
A miraculous survivor, this striking cathedral **(right)** was founded in 639, but underwent radical restructuring in 1008. It retains its Romanesque form, light-brick walls and an arcaded 9th-century portico.

② Doomsday Mosaics, Basilica
In these 12th–13th-century marvels, the Last Judgment **(above)** is dramatically depicted in superbly restored scenes of devils, angels, wild beasts and fires.

③ Apse Mosaics, Basilica
This moving 13th-century mosaic shows the Virgin in a blue robe with gold fringing, cradling her radiant child. Below are the 12 apostles standing in a meadow of flowers.

④ Iconostasis, Basilica
Marble panels show peacocks drinking at the fountain of eternal life

(left), small lions posing under a tree full of birds, while six columns support 15th-century paintings of the apostles with the Virgin.

⑤ Paving, Basilica
In vivid swirls of colours, rivalling the flooring in Basilica San Marco, are brilliant 11th-century tesserae of stone and glass. Cubes, semicircles and triangles are laid into square designs. The floor level was raised 30 cm (12 inches) during the basilica's reconstruction.

7 Campanile

The views from this simple 55-m (180-ft) bell tower **(left)** reach over the vast expanse of the lagoon, with its meandering canals and tidal flats, to the Adriatic Sea, Venice itself and even north to the Alps on a clear winter's day.

8 Throne of Attila

By popular belief this marble armchair **(below)** was the throne of the king of the Huns, though historical sources claim it was for the island's magistrates.

ATTILA THE HUN

The "Scourge of God", or the King of the Huns, ruled from 434 CE to 453 over an empire that stretched from the Alps and the Baltic towards the Caspian Sea. As part of his campaign against the Roman Empire, Attila attacked Milan, Verona and Padua, and refugees fled to Torcello. Burning the cathedral town of Aquileia gave him great satisfaction – his men raised a hill in Udine so he could enjoy the sight.

9 Museo dell'Estuario

An intriguing, if modest, collection of archaeological finds from the island and priceless treasures from the church are housed in the adjoining Gothic buildings.

NEED TO KNOW

MAP H1 ■ Boat line 12 from the Fondamente Nuove to Burano, then change to boat line 9

Basilica di Santa Maria dell' Assunta (Torcello Basilica): 041 730 119; open times vary, call ahead; adm €5 (€4 concessions); adm & audio guide €7 (€6 concessions)

Campanile: Open Mar–Oct: 10:30am–5:30pm daily;

Nov–Feb: 10am–5pm daily; adm €5; adm basilica and campanile €9 with audio guide

Santa Fosca: Open 10am–6pm Thu–Tue (from 9am Sun)

Museo dell'Estuario: 041 730 761; open times vary, call for details; closed public hols; adm €3 (€1.50 concessions); basilica and museum €8 (€6 concessions)

6 Santa Fosca

Alongside the basilica is this elegant church based on a Greek cross design, encircled by a five-sided colonnaded portico. The inside of the church is closed to visitors during services.

10 Locanda Cipriani

A favourite of American writer Ernest Hemingway, who stayed here *(see p148)* in 1948, this guesthouse **(left)** has a quiet charm that has attracted VIPs since it opened in 1938.

Campo Santa Margherita

This cheery, picturesque square in the district of Dorsoduro is a hive of activity day in, day out. It owes its name to the Christian martyr St Margaret of Antioch, possibly a fictitious figure, but highly popular in medieval times. Patron saint of expectant mothers, she is depicted in a niche on the square's northern wall with her emblem, the dragon. The square's capacious form, exploited by local children on bicycles and in-line skaters, is due to an enlargement project in the 1800s which opened up the south end by filling in canals.

1 Ex Chiesa di Santa Margherita

A writing 14th-century dragon symbolizing the martyrdom of the saint enlivens the foot of the bell tower of the former church. It has been restored by the university as the Auditorium Santa Margherita.

2 Palazzo Foscolo-Corner

This beautiful palace is virtually unchanged since the 1300s and instantly distinguishable by its deep overhanging eaves. A striking Byzantine-style lunette, bearing an inset with the family crest, tops the entrance portal.

3 Scuola Grande dei Carmini

Glorious rooms **(below)**, decorated with Tiepolo's masterpieces, are highlights of this confraternity. The upstairs ceiling shows *St Simon Stock Receiving the Scapular from the Virgin*.

Campo Santa Margherita

4 Calle del Forno

An unusual series of medieval-style projections from a first-floor dwelling, partly held up by brick columns, is one of the most interesting features of this busy thoroughfare leading to Piazzale Roma and the bus terminal. The street is named after a long-gone *forno* (bakery).

5 Scuola dei Varoteri

A splendid bas-relief of the Virgin sheltering a group of trades-men in adoration adorns the former tanners' guild dating from 1725. Because of its isolated position, it was once mistakenly thought to be the house of the city's executioner.

8 Chiesa di Santa Maria dei Carmini

This richly adorned church **(left)** survived Napoleon's suppression of the Carmelite order of monks in the adjoining monastery. Many of its 13th-century features are intact, such as the sculpted entrance porch.

RIO TERRÀ

Rio is a common name for canal, while *terrà* means filled-in. Dating back to the 1300s, the practice of filling in waterways was widespread in the 1800s to provide extra pedestrian space. Some were covered with low-slung arches to keep water flowing, exemplified by Via Garibaldi *(see p111)* in Castello. Later campaigns encouraged the reverse procedure.

9 Corte del Fondaco

A charming covered passageway leads through to this minor courtyard where curious, low, bricked-in arches indicate the former site of a 1700s flour store. The name *fondaco* – or store – is derived from the Arabic word *fonduq*.

10 Rio Nuovo

Excavated in 1932–3 to form a shortcut from Piazzale Roma to the Grand Canal, the canal has been closed to *vaporetti* since the 1990s, due to building damage.

6 The "House of the Moor"

Shakespeare's *Othello* was based on Cristoforo Moro, who was sent to govern Cyprus from 1508. This house at No. 2615 is his former home.

7 Altana Terraces

These timber roof platforms **(right)** were common in Venetian palaces, used by women for bleaching their hair in the sun. They are now used for laundry and partying on summer evenings, and can be seen around Campo Santa Margherita.

NEED TO KNOW

MAP K5

Scuola Grande dei Carmini, Dorsoduro: 041 528 94 20; open 10am–5pm daily; adm €7 (€5 concessions); www.scuolagrandecarmini.it

■ Numerous food outlets offering pizza slices and bars serving *tramezzini* (sandwiches) and *panini* (rolls) make for a cheap lunch option.

🔟 ⭐ Peggy Guggenheim Collection

The delightfully spacious, light-filled Collezione Peggy Guggenheim is home to works by more than 200 contemporary artists representing powerful avant-garde movements such as Cubism, Futurism and Surrealism. The landmark collection, put together by its far-sighted namesake, is housed in the 18th-century Palazzo Venier dei Leoni, known as the "unfinished palace" because of its one-storey construction. As well as the wonderful works of art on display inside the gallery, there is also a striking sculpture garden and the former home of Peggy Guggenheim to visit.

① The Poet
A wonderful starting point is this portrait (1911) by legendary Spanish artist Pablo Picasso (1881–1973), from his early Cubist period. The figure is executed from a limited palette of ochre and dark browns.

② Maiastra
This polished brass sculpture (1912) represents the magical bird who accompanies and protects the hero of Romanian fairy tales. Its creator was Romanian artist Constantin Brancusi (1876–1957).

③ Attirement of the Bride
This portrayal (1940) of an orange-robed bride assisted by mutant animals and humans **(below)** is by Max Ernst (1891–1976). The German Surrealist was married to Peggy Guggenheim from 1942 to 1946.

Peggy Guggenheim Collection

Key to Floorplan
- Gallery
- Nasher Sculpture Garden

Peggy Guggenheim Collection

4 Empire of Light

Magical light effects see darkened trees and a house silhouetted by a street lamp against a contrasting daytime sky with fluffy clouds in this work (1953–4) by René Magritte (1898–1967). The Belgian Surrealist was renowned for his eccentric subjects.

6 Woman Walking

This serene elongated form of a truncated female figure **(right)**, from 1932, apparently inspired by Etruscan design, is the recognized trademark of the Swiss artist Alberto Giacometti (1901–66), a short-term participant in the Surrealist movement.

7 The Moon Woman

This vibrant canvas (1942) starring a skeletal stick figure with an odd, padded curve is an early work by Jackson Pollock (1912–56), pre-dating his famous "drip" technique.

PEGGY GUGGENHEIM

This heir to a mining fortune (1898–1979) first came to Europe in 1921, quickly fitting into Bohemian Paris. Resolving to "buy a picture a day", she amassed a contemporary art collection before she made Venice her home in 1947. She is fondly remembered by locals here for her faithful dogs and for owning the city's last private gondola.

NEED TO KNOW

MAP D5 ■ Fondamenta Venier dei Leoni, Dorsoduro 704 (2nd entrance Calle S Cristoforo, Dorsoduro 701) ■ 041 240 54 11 ■ www.guggenheim-venice.it

Open 10am–6pm Wed–Mon (last admission 5:30pm); closed 25 Dec

Adm €17 (€14 over 65s, €9 students up to 26 years old); audio guides are available at the entrance for €7

■ For a light snack or a meal, head to the café.

■ Enjoy the view of the Grand Canal from the terrace.

■ Flash photography is not allowed.

9 Mobile

This simple master-piece of movement (1941) by Alexander Calder (1898–1976), which gave its name to all mobiles, hangs in the atrium of Guggenheim's house.

10 Angel of the City

Set on steps leading to the terrace, this bronze horse and rider (1948) by Italian sculptor Marino Marini (1901–80) greet passing boats.

5 Magic Garden

This deliberately child-like piece (1926) by Paul Klee (1879–1940) features blurry shapes and sketched-in faces and buildings.

8 Three Standing Figures

Beautifully placed in the Nasher Sculpture Garden, these sculptures (1953) by Henry Moore (1898–1986) were inspired by Italian bell towers.

The Top 10
of Everything

The world-famous Rialto Bridge, one of
four bridges spanning the Grand Canal

🔟 Moments in History

1 421 CE: Birth of Venice

Fleeing the Goths, who were looting their way southwards to Rome, the people of the Veneto sought refuge among the uninhabited islands of their marshy coast. There from the ashes of the Roman past rose the city of Venice. According to tradition on 25 March every year, the Church of San Giacometto is consecrated at Rialto. This is considered the founding date of the city.

The four bronze horses taken from Constantinople

2 697 CE: Electing the Doge

Soon after the surrounding coastal area and the lagoon was organized into a duchy, ruled by a "dux" or doge, nominated by the emperor in Constantinople. At the Basilica di San Marco (see pp12–15), the doge was presented to the city following his election. Paoluccio Anafesto was elected first doge.

3 1204: Siege of Constantinople

Led by the aged and blind doge Enrico Dandolo, the leaders of the Fourth Crusade agreed to attack the capital of Byzantium, as payment for warships supplied by Venice. The treasures taken include four gilded bronze horses. Replicas of the originals appear on the façade of Basilica di San Marco. The city fell in 1204, leaving Venice the ruler of Byzantium.

4 1378–81: Battle of Choggia

The long-standing rivalry between the maritime republics of Venice and Genoa turned into a naval battle in 1378. The attack culminated in 1381 when Venice defeated Genoa at Choggia to win undisputed maritime supremacy in the Adriatic and Mediterranean. The battle led to the Peace of Turin, which heralded the final decline of Genoese hegemony.

Genoese and Venetian naval warships at the Battle of Choggia

5 1571: Battle of Lepanto

At Lepanto, in Greece, the largest naval battle since antiquity witnessed an alliance of western powers inflict a devastating defeat on the Ottoman fleet.

6 1797: End of the Venetian Republic

After more than a millenium, the first Republic since antiquity fell in 1797 to the invading French troops of Napoleon Bonaparte.

7 1848: First Italian War of Independence

Led by Daniele Manin, the city revolted against Austrian domination, and the rebels proclaimed a new, but short-lived Republic, with the ultimate aim of joining a unified Italy. The city capitulated to the Austrians the following year, after a long siege.

Daniele Manin's statue, Campo Manin

8 1866: Austrian rule ends

The long military and political confrontation between Austria and the Italian states finally resulted in the unification of the Italian territories, including Venice and the Veneto.

9 1966: Floods devastate Venice

In November 1966, the city was hit by the worst floods in its history, sparking concern for the future of the city's delicate and decaying fabric.

10 2019: Floods threaten again

After more than 50 years, severe flooding left over 80 per cent of the city under water in November 2019.

TOP 10 FREQUENTLY ASKED QUESTIONS

A flooded *fondamenta*, Cannaregio

1 Is Venice still sinking?
Theoretically, the sinking came to a halt when the industries in Marghera stopped pumping out groundwater – it is the relative sea level that is rising.

2 What do the buildings stand on?
Pinewood piles overlaid with horizontal planks and marble-like Istrian stone slabs serve as the building foundation.

3 Is swimming in the canal allowed?
Swimming in the canal is forbidden and incurs a hefty fine.

4 How deep is the lagoon?
At its maximum depth, the lagoon is 15 m (49 ft) in the navigable channels dredged for shipping.

5 Is the sea safe for swimming?
Yes, periodic controls for bacterial counts are carried out.

6 Does everyone have a boat?
On average, one in two families possesses a pleasure boat.

7 Can you drink water from the drinking fountains?
Yes, it's the same as tap water and is subject to testing and treatment – bring your own water bottle to fill up.

8 How does the house numbering system work?
Within each of the six districts (*sestiere*), numbers follow the alleyways, taking in branch streets and courtyards.

9 What are the MOSE floodgates?
This dam project aims to protect Venice and its lagoon from high flood tides.

10 Why don't people restore the crumbling buildings?
Strict regulations concern façades, only porous stucco can be used as anything else tends to come away and is a hazard for passersby.

🔟 Venice Palaces

The striking façade of Ca' Rezzonico

1 Doge's Palace
See pp16–19.

2 Ca' d'Oro
The original lapis lazuli, vermilion and gold façade has long faded, but the breathtaking Gothic delicacy of this "golden palace" (see p103) is intact, with exquisite marble tracery and arcaded loggias crafted by 15th-century stonemasons.

Gothic architecture of Ca' d'Oro

3 Ca' Foscari
MAP L5 ■ Calle Foscari, Dorsoduro 3246 ■ Open for pre-booked guided tours only ■ www.unive.it

Set on a strategic bend of the Grand Canal, this excellent example of late Gothic architecture has a series of mullioned windows facing the water, surmounted by an Istrian stone frieze. Once home to the long-ruling Doge Francesco Foscari, today it is part of the University of Venice.

4 Ca' Rezzonico
MAP L5 ■ Fondamenta Rezzonico, Dorsoduro 3136 ■ Open 9am–6pm daily ■ Adm ■ www.visitmuve.it

This glittering palace adorned with Tiepolo ceiling frescoes, majestic Murano glass chandeliers and elaborate carved period furniture is now home to the Museum of 18th-century Venetian Life.

5 Palazzo Vendramin-Calergi
This stately Renaissance residence (see p67) built by known architects Lombardo and Coducci in the late 15th century was home to a string of noble families including the Cretan merchant Calergi in 1589. Another famed tenant was composer Richard Wagner, who spent his final years here. The palace is now home to the glittering City Casino.

6 Ca' Dario
Framed multicoloured round stones (tondi) embellish this privately owned, asymmetrical palace dating from 1486. Ca' Dario (see p25) was built for Giovanni Dario, who was an ambassador to Constantinople, where he negotiated a peace treaty that brought long-term hostilities between Venice and the Turks to a temporary halt.

7 Palazzo Mastelli

MAP D1 ■ Rio della Madonna dell'Orto, Cannaregio 3932 ■ Closed to public

This eclectic delight, on a peaceful back canal of Cannaregio, was the abode of three merchant brothers from Morea on the Peloponnese from 1112. Their turbaned likenesses in stone adorn neighbouring Campo dei Mori (see p104). Lions, birds and a prominent camel can be picked out on the Gothic façade.

8 Palazzi Contarini degli Scrigni e Corfu

MAP B5 ■ Calle Contarini Corfu, Dorsoduro 1057 ■ Closed to public

A 15th-century residence, enlarged by architect Vincenzo Scamozzi for the 17th-century proprietor Contarini "of the coffers" (scrigni), so-called for the vast wealth of his family. The roof-top "folly" acted as a useful observatory for astronomers.

9 Palazzo Barbaro

MAP M6 ■ Rio dell'Orso, S Marco 2840 ■ Closed to public

Cole Porter, Diaghilev, Monet and Whistler are just a few former guests of this private double palace, courtesy of the 19th-century Curtis family from Boston. Henry James (see p53) wrote The Aspern Papers here and used it as the setting for The Wings of a Dove.

10 Palazzo Pisani-Moretta

MAP M4 ■ Ramo Pisani e Barbarigo, S Polo 2766 ■ Open for private functions only

Venue of a fabulous masked ball during Carnival, when VIP guests glide up in gondolas to the candlelit Gothic façade on the Grand Canal. Tiepolo and Guarana contributed to the interior Baroque decorations.

Palazzo Pisani-Moretta

TOP 10 ARCHITECTURAL FEATURES OF A PALAZZO

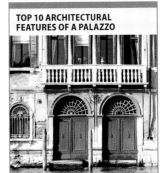

A typical canal entrance

1 Canal Entrance
This is where the family's private gondolas were moored and visitors were received.

2 Piano Nobile
The high-ceilinged first floor of a palazzo hosts the sumptuous salons and family's living quarters.

3 Façade
Usually fronting a canal, this was the only exterior wall decorated with a costly stone overlay to impress visitors.

4 Funnel-Shaped Chimneys
These and many other variations punctuate rooftops, their long shafts often running along outside walls.

5 Kitchen
This was always located on the ground floor for practical reasons.

6 Central Well
This received filtered rain water for the palazzo's main water supply.

7 Entrance Portal
The importance of the main entrance was usually indicated by the distinctive family crest.

8 Enclosed Courtyard
This bustling area, usually with store rooms, was often used for the family's business transactions.

9 Altana Roof Terrace-Platform
These open-air areas were traditionally used for hanging out the washing or bleaching hair in the sun.

10 Land Access
Private gondolas rendered this relatively unimportant and hence, a narrow alley sufficed in its stead.

⭐🔟 Venice Churches

① Basilica di San Marco
See pp12–15.

② Santa Maria Gloriosa dei Frari
See pp32–3.

Mosaic floor, Santi Giovanni e Paolo

③ Santi Giovanni e Paolo
MAP E3 ■ Campo SS Giovanni e Paolo, Castello ■ Open 9am–6pm Mon–Sat, noon–6pm Sun ■ Adm ■ www.santigiovanniepaolo.it

The monumental tombs of 25 doges take pride of place in this Gothic giant, built by Dominican friars from the 13th to 15th centuries. Among them is the tribute to Pietro Mocenigo for his valorous struggle to defend Venice's eastern colonies against the Turks (west wall). Inside are numerous works of art including splendid paintings by Veronese and a polyptych (1465) by Giovanni Bellini.

④ Santa Maria dei Miracoli
A favourite among Venetians for weddings, Pietro Lombardo's showcase (1481–9) is resplendent again after restoration to deal with rising damp. The problem is not new – in Renaissance times marble slabs were affixed to the brick exterior with a cavity left for air flow. The ceiling gleams with gilt miniatures of holy figures *(see p104)*.

⑤ San Zaccaria
MAP F4 ■ Campo S Zaccaria, Castello ■ Open 10am–noon & 4–6pm Mon–Sat, 4–6pm Sun & public hols ■ Adm (chapels & crypt)

An intricately decorated 15th-century façade by Coducci and, inside, Giovanni Bellini's superb *Madonna and Saints* (1505) are highlights of this 9th-century church. The adjoining convent, now a police station, used to host puppet shows to entertain the nuns.

⑥ San Giorgio Maggiore
MAP F5 ■ Isola di S Giorgio Maggiore ■ Open Apr–Oct: 9am–7pm daily; Nov–Mar: 8:30am–6pm daily ■ Adm (bell tower)

Palladio's harmoniously proportioned church (1566–1610), inspired by Greek temple design, stands across the water from Piazza San Marco. The interior is offset by two dynamic paintings by Tintoretto from 1594, *The Last Supper* and *Gathering the Manna*, on the chancel walls. The bell tower offers views over Venice. Don't miss the monks' Gregorian chants every Sunday at 11am.

⑦ Santa Maria della Salute
MAP D5 ■ Campo della Salute, Dorsoduro ■ Open 9am–noon & 3–5:30pm daily ■ Adm (sacristy)

A great Baroque church dominating the southernmost entrance to the Grand Canal, Santa Maria della Salute's silhouette has become one of Venice's most well-known landmarks. Designed by architect Longhena in 1630, it has a spacious interior, while the altar houses a precious Byzantine icon. Dramatic works by Titian and Tintoretto can be appreciated in the sacristy.

8 Chiesa di San Sebastiano

Renaissance painter Paolo Veronese (1528–88) spent a large proportion of his life joyously decorating the ceiling, walls, organ doors and altar of this unassuming 16th-century church (see p98), and was buried among his colourful masterpieces.

9 Madonna dell'Orto

MAP D1 ■ Campo Madonna dell'Orto, Cannaregio ■ Open 10am–5pm Mon–Sat, noon–5pm Sun ■ Adm ■ http://events.veneziaunica.it

Eleven huge canvases by devout parishioner Tintoretto enhance this graceful Gothic church. Two masterpieces flank the high altar – the gruesome *The Last Judgment* and the soaring grandeur of *The Making of the Golden Calf*, both thought to have been painted about 1563.

Façade of Madonna dell'Orto

10 San Pantalon

MAP K4 ■ Campo S Pantalon, Dorsoduro ■ Open 10am–12:30pm & 3:30–6pm Mon–Thu, 10am–noon & 3:30–7pm Sat, 9am–12:30pm & 3:30–6pm Sun ■ www.sanpantalon.it

Two treasures lurk behind a ramshackle façade: a nail from the True Cross and the overwhelming ceiling (1680–1704) by Gian Antonio Fumiani, a labour of love that ended when he purportedly plunged to his death.

TOP 10 SHRINES AND TABERNACLES

Flowers at a shrine to St Anthony

1 St Anthony
MAP D2 ■ Calle Larga, Cannaregio
This 1668 "wardrobe" is full of fresh flower offerings.

2 Sottoportego de la Madonna
MAP D3 ■ Sant' Aponal, S Polo
Pope Alexander III took refuge here from Emperor Barbarossa in 1177.

3 Gondolier's Shrine
MAP R5 ■ Ponte della Paglia, S Marco
A 1583 Madonna greets boats approaching the bridge.

4 Corte Nova
MAP G4 ■ Castello
Painted images over a lace-trimmed mantlepiece.

5 Covered Passageway
MAP F4 ■ Calle Zorzi, Castello
The Virgin's protection has been implored here against plague and enemy attacks.

6 Scuola Grande della Misericordia
MAP D2 ■ Cannaregio
Carvings of laden boats seek protection for the ferries, which set out from here.

7 Corte de Ca' Sarasina
MAP H5 ■ Castello
Shrine dating back to the 1600s in memory of the dead.

8 Ponte del Fontego
MAP F3 ■ Campo S Giustina, Castello
A Neo-Classical bridge featuring gondola bas-reliefs.

9 Gondola Traghetto Point
MAP L4 ■ S Tomà, S Polo
Madonna on a pole in the Grand Canal.

10 Boatmen's Pole
Tabernacle midway on the San Giuliano–Venice channel.

🔟 Famous Venetians

1 Marco Polo

Legendary Cathay and the kingdom of the mighty Kublai Khan took pride of place in the explorer Marco Polo's best-selling account of his 20-year odyssey to the Far East, *Book of the Marvels of the World*. Son of a Venetian merchant, Polo (1254–1324) is responsible for the introduction of pasta and window blinds to the western world.

Marco Polo

2 Antonio Vivaldi

Vivaldi (1678–1741) was both an accomplished musician and an influential Baroque composer. Of his 500 concertos, *The Four Seasons* is the best known. J S Bach was a noted fan and transcribed ten of the Italian's concertos. Vivaldi spent extended periods teaching music at the Pietà home (see p109) for girls.

3 Giacomo Casanova

This marvellous romantic figure (1725–98) was variously a diplomat, scholar, trainee priest, adventurer, gambler, notary's clerk, violinist, womanizer, exile, millionaire, writer and spy. Casanova was imprisoned in the Doge's Palace (see pp16–19) on charges of being a magician, from where he effected an infamously daring escape.

Giacomo Casanova

4 Claudio Monteverdi

This late Renaissance madrigalist (1567–1643) is attributed with the introduction of the solo voice to theatre. His opera *Proserpina Rapita* was the first to be performed in Venice. After long periods at the court of the Gonzagas, he accepted an appointment at the Basilica di San Marco and worked for the Scuola Grande di San Rocco (see p89).

5 John Cabot

Italian navigator Giovanni Caboto, or John Cabot (1450–99), and his sons were authorized by Henry VII of England to search for new lands with the aim of furthering trade. Believing himself on the north-east coast of Asia, he landed on Newfoundland in Canada and claimed it for England, opening up cod fishing.

6 Elena Lucrezia Corner Piscopia

It was inconceivable for the church in 1678 that a woman should teach religion, so the University of Padua awarded this child prodigy and the first female graduate (1646–84) a degree in philosophy, instead of one in theology to which she aspired.

7 Daniele Manin

Organizer of the 1848 rebellion against Austrian rule, the Venetian patriot (1804–57) is commemorated by a statue in Campo Manin. An independent "republic" was declared and survived 17 months of bombardments and even cholera, concluding with Manin's exile to Paris.

8 Paolo Sarpi

In 1509 when the pope excommunicated Venice for insubordination, which involved restrictions on church construction and the refusal to hand over two priests on criminal charges, Sarpi (1552–1623) resolved the rupture.

A patriot and theologian, he was an advocate of division between State and Church.

Caterina Cornaro

⑨ Caterina Cornaro

This Venetian noblewoman (1454–1510) married the king of Cyprus then allegedly poisoned him, thus securing the strategic island for Venice. Her return to the city was an occasion of great pomp, recalled to this day in a waterborne procession during the Regata Storica *(see p77)*. Cornaro's reward was the hilltown of Asolo.

⑩ Luigi Nono

This musician (1924–90) made milestone progress in the field of electronic music, and an archive named after him was set up in Venice in 1993. A committed Communist, his works were often provocative.

Avant-garde composer Luigi Nono

TOP 10 FOREIGN COMMUNITIES

Artist Claude Monet's painting
Le Grand Canal

1 French
Impressionist painter Claude Monet and writers Théophile Gautier and Marcel Proust were attracted to the city in the late 1800s.

2 Greeks
Here since 1498, the Greeks are the longest surviving group, still active with their own church.

3 Armenians
Fleeing Turkish invasion, in 1717 the close-knit religious group was granted an island by the Republic *(see p124)*.

4 Dalmatians (Slavs)
Traders from a historical region of Croatia, whose boats gave their name to the Riva degli Schiavoni *(see p109)*.

5 Turks
Although the Turks were enemies of Venice, the Republic still rented them a trade centre between 1621 and 1898.

6 Jews
The Spanish Inquisition triggered the move here for many Jews expelled from other European countries.

7 Albanians
Calle degli Albanesi near Piazza San Marco is named in honour of this large 15th-century community.

8 Germans
The former German trade headquarters Fondaco dei Tedeschi attracted artists such as Albrecht Dürer.

9 British
Extended sojourns here were de rigueur for the British upper class during the 19th-century Grand Tour.

10 Americans
Leading literary figures and patrons of the arts have paid long-term visits since the 19th century.

🔟 Writers and Venice

Teatro Comunale Carlo Goldoni

1 Carlo Goldoni
"Italy's Molière" (1707–93) is celebrated at the Venetian theatre named in his honour (see p65). Performances of his lively, witty comedies are staged in Venetian dialect and peopled with recognizable local characters. The prolific playwright moved to Paris and was rewarded with a royal pension, but he died destitute due to the French Revolution.

2 Thomas Mann
The sombre 1912 novel *Death in Venice* was both written and set in Venice and the Lido resort by the German Nobel Prize-winner (1875–1955). It tells the story of an ageing writer in dire need of relaxation who visits the city, but in the wake of an impossible infatuation slowly succumbs to the spreading cholera epidemic and dies.

3 William Shakespeare
Although he never visited Italy, let alone Venice, the English Bard (1564–1616) used accounts by contemporary travellers for the plots of *The Merchant of Venice* and *Othello*, portraying a city buzzing with trade and intrigue. *Romeo and Juliet* is set in nearby Verona (see p130).

William Shakespeare

4 Thomas Coryate
The very first traveller to write a detailed description of Venice in English, this eccentric gentleman from Somerset, England (1577–1617) compiled *Crudities, with Observations of Venice* (1611): "Such is the rarenesse of the situation of Venice, that it doth even amaze and drive into admiration all strangers that upon their first arrival behold the same."

5 Johann Wolfgang von Goethe
The story goes that this German literary giant (1749–1832) had his first ever view of the sea from Venice's Campanile. His first visit to the city and Italy was an experience of personal renewal. The account, published as *Italian Journey* (1786–8), is considered an early classic of travel literature.

Johann Wolfgang von Goethe

6 Lord Byron
Eccentricities such as a menagerie of foxes and monkeys, not to mention swimming feats in the Grand Canal, made the English Romantic poet (1788–1824) something of a legend during his three-year sojourn here. His Venice-inspired work included *The Two Foscari* and the fourth canto of his autobiographical work *Childe Harold's Pilgrimage*.

7 John Ruskin
The meticulous, if opinionated, labour of love of this British art critic (1819–1900), *The Stones of Venice*, was the first work to focus the attention of visitors on the city's unique architectural heritage

and Gothic style, as opposed to the art. The book was largely the outcome of an 1849 visit to the city.

8 Henry James

The leitmotif of this US novelist (1843–1916) was the contrast between what he saw as the spontaneity of the Americas and the staidness of Europe. Between 1872 and 1909 he compiled *Italian Hours*, a "travel diary", with plenty of comments on Venice.

Ernest Hemingway

9 Ernest Hemingway

This US Nobel Prize-winner (1899–1961) experienced Italy as a volunteer ambulance driver in World War I (recounted in *A Farewell to Arms*) and was wounded near Treviso. *Across the River and into the Trees* is set in Harry's Bar (see p25).

10 Charles Dickens

The great English novelist (1812–70) spent a brief period in Venice during a tour of Italy, and the city inspired a dream sequence in his work *Pictures from Italy* (1846).

Illustration from "An Italian Dream" in Dickens's *Pictures from Italy*

TOP 10 BACKGROUND READS

***Death in Venice* film adaptation**

1 Death in Venice, Thomas Mann
A portrayal of desire and decadence amid the fog.

2 Venice, Jan Morris
An expert account of the delights of the city and its maritime history.

3 Venice, an Anthology Guide, Milton Grundy
A guide around town, seen through the eyes of famous writers.

4 Ruskin's Venice, editor Arnold Whittick
A very readable version of Ruskin's landmark work.

5 Stone Virgin, Barry Unsworth
A mystery involving the 15th-century statue of a famous courtesan.

6 Histoire de ma Vie, Giacomo Casanova
Autobiography detailing his famous escape (see p50).

7 Dead Lagoon, Michael Dibdin
Detective Aurelio Zen navigates Venice's murky waters fraught with unease and intrigue.

8 The Architecture of Venice, Deborah Howard
An unbeatable architectural classic.

9 Stabat Mater, Tiziano Scarpa
Set in the Ospedale della Pietà, Venice's music school, at the beginning of the 18th century.

10 Acqua Alta, Donna Leon
From the best-selling mystery series featuring detective Guido Brunetti.

🔟 Artists in Venice

The Madonna of the Meadow (1505) by Giovanni Bellini

1 Giovanni Bellini

Giovanni Bellini (1430–1516), with his father Jacopo and brother Gentile, made Venice one of the greatest centres of Renaissance art. His anatomy studies added great precision to his work. His trademarks are radiant Madonnas, serene St Peters and brilliant satiny robes.

2 Canaletto (Giovanni Antonio Canal)

Famous for his landscapes of Venice and England, Canaletto (1697–1768) thrived under the patronage of the British consul Joseph Smith. Unfortunately, very few of his paintings can be seen in Venice.

3 Titian (Tiziano Vecellio)

A native of the Cadore region, whose awe-inspiring Dolomite peaks often feature in his highly coloured dynamic compositions, Titian (1488–1576) came to Venice when young and studied under Giovanni Bellini.

4 Jacopo Tintoretto

The great Mannerist of the late Renaissance, Tintoretto (1518–94) produced huge, glowing canvases, seen at his main showcase the Scuola Grande di San Rocco (see p89), as well as his parish church Madonna dell'Orto (see p49).

5 Paolo Veronese

Foremost painter of the Venetian School, Veronese (1528–88) created huge canvases in classical settings and teeming with people. They are on display in the Doge's Palace (see pp16–19) and the Chiesa di San Sebastiano (see p98).

6 Marietta Robusti

Known as "la Tintoretta", Robusti (1554–1590) was the illegitimate daughter of Tintoretto and, dressed as a boy, followed her father

View of the Grand Canal (late 1720s) by Canaletto

to his workshop. The only painting conclusively attributed to her is a self-portrait in the Uffizi Gallery in Florence. She is buried in Madonna dell'Orto (see p49), where Tintoretto also lies.

7 Vittorio Carpaccio

This Renaissance master (1465–1525) delighted in remarkably detailed scenes of daily life in contemporary Venice. His original narrative style and marvellous command of light characterize his many cycles on display at the Accademia galleries (see p31) and the Scuola di San Giorgio degli Schiavoni (see p57).

8 Giorgione

A native of Castelfranco Veneto, Giorgione (1477–1510) came to Venice when young to serve as an apprentice under Giovanni Bellini. In his brief life, he produced memorable mood works that he never signed. One of his most famous

Virgin and Child (1504) by Giorgione

works, *The Tempest*, can be seen in the Accademia (see p30).

9 Pietro Longhi

Longhi (1702–85) painted witty scenes of the everyday life of the well-to-do folk in Venice. Examples of his work can be admired at the Fondazione Querini Stampalia (see p56), as well as in Ca' Rezzonico (see p46). Many figures are wearing the traditional Venetian mask.

10 Rosalba Carriera

A Venetian Rococo portraitist, Carriera (1673–1757) was the most appreciated miniaturist of her time, with her work adorning snuff boxes. Her subjects included mythological and allegorical figures as well as portraits from everyday life. She also pioneered the use of pastels.

TOP 10 VENICE ARCHITECTS

Chiesa del Santissimo Redentore, by Andrea Palladio

1 Andrea Palladio (1508–80)
Regarded as one of the most influential architects of the western world, Palladio designed Classical villas in the Veneto and churches in Venice.

2 Jacopo Sansovino (1486–1570)
Outstanding architect who trained under – and took his name from – sculptor Andrea Sansovino. Examples of Jacopo's work are the Libreria (see p22) and Zecca.

3 Baldassare Longhena (1598–1682)
Longhena's masterpiece, Santa Maria della Salute, was designed when he was just 26, but his flamboyant style is also seen in Ca' Rezzonico (see p46).

4 Pietro Lombardo (1435–1515)
Lombardy native Pietro was director of works at the Doge's Palace. His trademark leafy bas-relief pattern is also seen at Santa Maria dei Miracoli (see p104).

5 Mauro Coducci (c.1440–1504)
The Renaissance designs of Lombardy native Coducci can be seen in Palazzo Vendramin-Calergi (see p67).

6 Bartolomeo Bon (1374–1464)
Sculptor/architect Bon's designs were the basis for the church and Scuola di San Rocco and the Ca' d'Oro (see p46).

7 Michele Sanmicheli (1484–1559)
Original military fortification designs by this Mannerist architect are found in his home town of Verona.

8 Antonio Da Ponte (1512–95)
This engineer and architect is well known for the Rialto Bridge (see p58).

9 Giannantonio Selva (1757–1819)
In Venice, Selva is best known for the elegant Fenice theatre (see p64).

10 Carlo Scarpa (1906–78)
Modernist Scarpa reorganized both the Accademia and the Querini Stampalia along Japanese-inspired lines.

TOP 10 Museums and Galleries

1 Accademia Galleries
See pp30–31.

2 Museo del Merletto
MAP H1 ▪ Piazza Baldassare Galuppi 187, Burano ▪ Open 10am–4pm Tue–Sun (last admission 3:30pm) ▪ Adm ▪ museo merletto.visitmuve.it

A must for craft-lovers is the lacemaking island of Burano and this precious display of more than 200 rare lace items, documenting a 500-year history.

3 Museo del Vetro
MAP G2 ▪ Fondamenta Giustiniani 8, Murano ▪ Open 10am–5pm daily (last admission 4pm) ▪ Adm ▪ www. visitmuve.it

A phenomenal chandelier from 1864, constructed with 356 handmade pieces, weighing 330 kg (730 lb) and measuring nearly 7 m (23 ft) in circumference and 4-m (13-ft) high, is the star of this glass museum in the Palazzo Giustiniani. Other exhibits include Phoenician phials, blown vases, ruby chalices,

Murano glassware at Museo del Vetro

exquisite mirrors and the famed kaleidoscopic beads that were once traded worldwide.

4 Palazzo Grassi
This collection (see p82) of contemporary art, housed in a palace on the Grand Canal, is renewed on a regular basis. The inspirational sister gallery is Punta della Dogana (see p98).

5 Fondazione Querini Stampalia
MAP R4 ▪ Campo S Maria Formosa, Castello 5252 ▪ Open 10am–6pm Tue–Sun (last admission 5:30pm) ▪ Adm ▪ www.querini stampalia.org

This unmissable Renaissance palace was the bequest of Giovanni Querini in 1868, the last member of the illustrious dynasty, on the condition that the library be made avail-able "particularly in the evenings for the conveni-ence of scholars". The immaculately restored palace-museum houses fascinating scenes of public and private life by Gabriel Bella and Pietro Longhi, as well as Carlo Scarpa's Modernist creations.

6 Museo Correr

A tremendous number of priceless artworks and a miscellany of items on Venice's history are housed in this fine museum *(see p22)* on Piazza San Marco.

Striking decor of Museo Correr

7 Ca' Pesaro Galleria d'Arte Moderna

MAP N1 ▪ Fondamenta Ca' Pesaro, S Croce 2076 ▪ Open 10am–5pm Tue–Sun (last admission 4pm) ▪ Adm ▪ www.visitmuve.it

A Baroque triumph of a palace, Ca' Pesaro's interior, in contrast, houses works by European 19th- and 20th-century masters such as Marc Chagall and Gustave Klimt, includng a strong collection of Italian works.

November 1870 by Telemaco Signorini in the Ca' Pesaro Galleria

8 Scuola di San Giorgio degli Schiavoni

MAP F4 ▪ Calle dei Furlani, Castello 3259 ▪ Open 10am–5:30pm Wed–Mon ▪ Adm ▪ www.scuoladalmatavenezia.com

The finest works by Vittorio Carpaccio can be seen at the confraternity of the Slavs (Schiavoni). *Slaying The Dragon* is one of the scenes from the lives of Dalmatian saints, which were painted between 1502 and 1507.

9 Scuola Grande di San Rocco

The San Rocco *(see p89)* confraternity has been turned into a gallery to display its spectacular collection of works by Tintoretto. The artist won the commission hands down – not content with a sketch, he completed an entire canvas. He then spent 23 years devoting himself to the cycle of 60 inspired Old and New Testament scenes, culminating in the breathtaking *Crucifixion* (1565). These masterpieces are the crowning glory of Tintoretto's life work.

Doge's barge, Museo Storico Navale

10 Museo Storico Navale

MAP G4 ▪ Campo S Biagio, Castello 2148 ▪ Open 11am–5pm Wed–Mon ▪ Adm ▪ www.visitmuve.it

Watercraft galore are found here, and almost an entire floor is dedicated to the naval history of the Venetian Republic's naval past. However, the highlight is the replica of the Doge's ceremonial barge, *Bucintoro*, decorated with allegorical statues.

TOP 10 Bridges

Stone bridge with three arches, Ponte dei Tre Archi

1 Ponte dei Tre Archi
MAP B1

A favourite subject for artists, this unusual three-arched high bridge dating from 1688 crosses the Cannaregio canal close to where it joins the lagoon. It was the work of engineer Andrea Tirali, nicknamed Tiranno (the tyrant) by his employees.

2 Rialto Bridge
MAP P3

The design of this most famous Venetian bridge (see p34) at the narrowest point of the Grand Canal was hotly contested – leading 16th-century architects Michelangelo, Sansovino and Palladio entered the competition, but lost out to Antonio da Ponte. There were two previous bridges on this site; a flimsy timber bridge that collapsed in 1444 under the weight of a crowd, then a drawbridge, which would be raised for the passage of tall-masted sailing ships.

3 Bridge of Sighs
MAP R5

This evocatively named bridge (see p17) (known as Ponte dei Sospiri in Italian) once led convicts from the beautiful Doge's Palace to the horrors of the adjacent prisons.

4 Ponte degli Scalzi
MAP J1

One of the city's most marvellous lookout points, over fascinating palaces and boats, can be found at the highest point of this elegant 40-m- (130-ft-) long bridge, which rises 7 m (23 ft) above the Grand Canal. Named after the nearby monastery of bare-footed monks, this 1934 structure in Istrian stone by Eugenio Miozzi replaced an Austrian-built iron bridge.

Overview of Ponte della Libertà

 Ponte della Libertà
MAP A1

Truth and irony combine in the name of this 3.6-km (2-mile) "Bridge of Freedom": the first full link between the mainland and Venice was put in place in 1933, when Italy was living under Fascism. The construction was preceded 86 years earlier by the Austrian-built railway bridge across the lagoon. Before that, the city relied entirely on boats.

 Ponte dei Pugni
MAP K5

Pugni (fistfights) between rival clans took place here until 1705 when they were outlawed for their violence. Stone footprints marked the starting point of the combat, but contestants usually ended up in the canal.

 Bridge with No Parapet
MAP D2

One of only two remaining bridges with no side protection, this one spans a quiet side canal in Cannaregio. The other is the Ponte del Diavolo on Torcello.

 Ponte delle Tette
MAP M2

When an increase in the practice of sodomy was recorded in the 1400s, the city's prostitutes were encouraged to display their feminine wares at the windows over the "Bridge of Breasts".

 Tre Ponti
MAP B3

Not three but five interlocking bridges span the Rio Novo canal near Piazzale Roma. The timber and stone structures afford views taking in 13 other bridges.

Tre Ponti three-way bridge

 Ponte della Costituzione
MAP B3

Also known as the Ponte di Calatrava, after its designer Santiago Calatrava, this fourth Grand Canal is modelled on a gondola's hull. It has attracted criticism since its 2008 inauguration due its minimalist modern design and the high cost of construction.

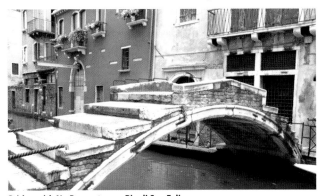

Bridge with No Parapet, over Rio di San Felice

Off the Beaten Track

1 Pinacoteca Manfrediniana

MAP E6 ■ Dorsoduro 1
■ Open 10am–1pm & 3–5pm
Thur–Fri, Sat 10am–6pm ■ Adm
■ www.manfrediana.it

This museum owes its name to the marquis Federico Manfredini, whose paintings and prints were donated to Venice. The displays here include works by Bellini, Cima da Conegliano, Lippi and Vivarini.

2 Rio Terrà Rampani

MAP M2 ■ San Polo

Just around the corner from Ponte delle Tette, "Bridge of Breasts", (see p59) is this quiet thoroughfare. Referred to as the "Carampane" (Ca' Rampani), it was where sex workers were based in the Venetian Republic. The city had some 11,600 officially registered courtesans in the 1500s.

3 Sant'Elena

MAP H6

Located in the far eastern extremity of Venice, this quiet resi-dential islet has marvellous shady

Sant'Elena

parkland on the waterfront. Children can enjoy the skating rink and playground while parents relax at laidback cafés.

4 Celestia to Bacini Walkway

MAP G3 ■ Castello

This unusual walkway clings to a perimeter wall of the ancient Arsenale shipyard in a rather neglected zone of Castello. It makes for an atmospheric walk, offering marvellous views over the lagoon and leading to a cluster of old workers' dwellings.

5 Corte dell'Anatomia

MAP L2 ■ S Croce

This peaceful courtyard was named after the anatomy theatre that existed here in 1368. Much later, in 1671, in neighbouring Campo San Giacomo dell'Orio, a College of Anatomy was established in what is now a separate building with an attractive trellis draped with vines.

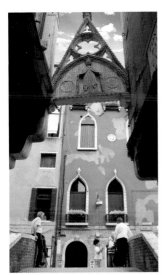

Vibrant Calle del Paradiso

6 Calle del Paradiso
MAP R3 ▪ Castello, San Lio

This attractive alley just off the busy San Lio thoroughfare is lined with medieval-style overhangs, as well as restaurants and shops. The name comes from the delightful lopsided, sculptured 15th-century arch depicting the Virgin and her devotees at the end.

7 Campo dei Gesuiti
MAP E2 ▪ Cannaregio

A favourite spot for children to play in, this is a spacious neighbourhood square. In addition to the Gesuiti (Jesuit) church, it is flanked by the cavernous Crociferi complex, erstwhile monastery, then barracks, now student lodgings. Wander inside to admire the cloisters and the canal-side café.

8 Corte del Duca Sforza
MAP L6 ▪ San Marco

This picturesque courtyard, which opens on to the Grand Canal, is surprisingly well hidden. It takes its name from the Duke of Milan who took over a partially constructed palace here in 1461, though work went no further than the diamond-point ashlar on the façade. The artist Titian used the building as a studio while he was working on the Doge's Palace (see pp16–19).

9 Campo della Celestia
MAP G3 ▪ Castello

Now a tranquil residential spot, back in the 1200s this square saw plenty of comings and goings due to the riotous behaviour of the sisters in the Cistercian convent. The first archive of city affairs was established here under Napoleon.

10 Campo della Maddalena
MAP D2 ▪ Cannaregio

Just off the main thoroughfare Strada Nova, you will find this beautiful raised square. It is often used as a film location, due to the fact that it has remained all but unchanged since medieval times. Its modest houses are topped with a fascinating range of chimneys.

Unspoilt and appealing Campo della Maddalena

🔟 Children's Attractions

The Giardini in Castello, a great place for children to let off steam

1 Play Areas

Children tired of art and architecture can release their energy at well-equipped playgrounds with slides, swings and frames at Parco Savorgnan near Ponte delle Guglie in Cannaregio and the fenced-in waterfront park at Giardini in Castello *(see p111)*. The vast shady green expanse of Sant'Elena even has a modest skating rink and an artificial climbing wall. Otherwise, make friends with the city kids as they kick footballs or cycle around Campo San Polo on an afternoon.

2 Ferry Trips

Restful for adults, exciting for youngsters, the varied boat lines are an ideal way for families to appreciate the joys of the city. Get older children to plan trips on the route maps, but avoid the outside seating on the *vaporetto* with toddlers. For an extended trip, take the majestic double-decker *motonave* over to Lido and Punta Sabbioni *(see p119)*.

3 Glassmaking Demonstrations

Great time is guaranteed as children are transfixed by crafters blowing blobs of molten glass into fine vases, or moulding coloured rods into myriad animal shapes. Small workshops are dotted all over Venice, while Murano *(see p117)* has more large-scale furnaces – demonstrations are free, on the condition that you stroll through the showroom afterwards.

4 Museo di Storia Naturale

MAP L1 ■ Salizzada del Fondaco dei Turchi, S Croce 1730 ■ 041 275 02 06 ■ Open 9am–5pm daily (last admission an hour before closing) ■ Adm ■ www.visitmuve.it

Housed in a palazzo on the Grand Canal, this museum covers over 700 million years of history with its two million-plus objects. The collection is organized into three sections: paleotology, exploration and nature. The highlight is a 3.6-m- (12-ft-) tall, 7-m- (23-ft-) long skeleton of the dinosaur *Ouranosaurus nigeriensis*.

Museo di Storia Naturale

Boat in the Museo Storico Navale

5 Museo Storico Navale

Easily the best city museum (see p57) for children, this three-floor haven of shipbuilding includes Chinese junks and exhibits from World War II, such as the famed torpedoes guided by Italian Navy divers, responsible for sinking British warships.

6 Peggy Guggenheim Collection

Every Sunday the museum (see pp40–41) hosts Art4Family, free educational workshops in English and Italian, run by artists and students from the Venice Academy of Fine Arts, for children aged 4 to 10 and their parents. You must book in advance.

7 Ca' Macana

MAP K6 ■ Calle delle Botteghe, Dorsoduro 3172

This mask shop (see p72) offers short courses that are both fun and stimulating. Experienced instructors share their craft by explaining the time-honoured techniques of the Venetian mask-making tradition. Participants can choose from over 60 styles to make masks.

8 Doge's Palace Prisons and Armoury

Children are thrilled by the spooky labyrinth of narrow passageways through the palace's (see pp16–19) erstwhile prisons, and it's fun deciphering the graffiti scratched on the walls by inmates over the centuries. In the armoury,

hunt out the unusual child-sized suit from the 16th century, along with the protection for horses.

9 Mistero e Magia

MAP R4 ■ Ruga Giuffa, Castello 4925 ■ Closed Sun

Run by a real magician, this shop is full of essentials such as wands, hats, and books revealing the tricks of the trade in Italian and English.

10 Visiting the Lido

If younger children are starting to tire of the galleries and museums, take them to play at the Lido (see pp122–5). The free beaches offer hours of fun and not just in the summer. Bikes can also be hired.

Visitors relaxing at the Beach, Lido

🔟 Entertainment Venues

Stunning interior of Teatro La Fenice

1 Teatro La Fenice

MAP N5 ■ Tickets from Venezia Unica offices at the theatre (041 2424) or online ■ www.teatrolafenice.it

This glorious theatre (see p81) hosts world-famous opera and concert performances. It was re-inaugurated in December 2003. Productions range from Verdi and Rossini to contemporary composers.

2 Teatro Malibran

MAP Q2 ■ Corte del Teatro Malibran, Cannaregio ■ Tickets from Venezia Unica offices at the theatre (041 2424)

In a quiet square near Rialto stands the Malibran Theatre, re-inaugurated in 2001 to take on part of the Fenice's productions. Dating back to 1678 as Teatro Grimani, it was renamed after the 19th-century Spanish mezzo-soprano Maria Malibran.

Teatro Malibran

3 Films in English

MAP M1 ■ Videoteca Pasinetti: Salizzada San Stae, Santa Croce 1990; 041 274 71 40; www.comune.venezia. it ■ Venice Film Festival: 041 521 87 11; www.labiennale.org

The Venice Film Library occasionally shows films in English during the winter. In late summer the local cinemas screen some of the highlights from the Venice Film Festival.

4 Palazzo Barbarigo Minotto

MAP D5 ■ Fondamenta Duodo o Barbarigo, San Marco 2504 ■ 340 971 72 72 ■ www.musicapalazzo.com

A great way to experience grand operas, Musica a Palazzo performs each act of an opera in a different hall of the grand Palazzo Barbarigo Minotto. The travelling opera is a revival of a tradition that began at the end of the 19th century.

5 Vivaldi Concerts

MAP F4 ■ Chiesa della Pietà, Riva degli Schiavoni, Castello ■ 045 800 64 11 ■ www.chiesavivaldi.it

Performances of Vivaldi's *Four Seasons* by I Virtuosi Italiani can be enjoyed in the church where it was composed. Designed by Giorgio Massari with the guidance of Vivaldi himself, the remarkable acoustics and frescoes by Tiepolo make for an inspiring experience.

6 Chamber Music

MAP M6 ■ Campo S Vidal, San Marco 2862 ■ 041 277 05 61 ■ www.interpreti veneziani.com

While listening to the uplifting notes of Vivaldi's *Four Seasons* or a masterpiece from Bach or Benedetto Marcello, this is the perfect spot to take a moment to unwind and relax from the day's hectic sightseeing. The Church of San Vidal was rebuilt around 1700 and has a spacious interior.

7 Concerts in Costume
MAP J5 ■ Scuola Grande dei Carmini, Campo S Margherita, Dorsoduro ■ 041 528 76 67 ■ www.musicainmaschera.com

Talented young singers and musicians perform comic operas at the Scuola Grande dei Carmini (see p38). It makes for a memorable evening.

8 Palazzetto Bru Zane
MAP L2 ■ S Polo 2368 ■ 041 30 376 ■ www.bru-zane.com

Housed in the ornate 17th-century Palazzetto Bru Zane, the Centre for French Romantic Music hosts concerts of French chamber music and symphonic and choral works dating between 1780 and 1920. It also organizes lectures and educational events.

9 Auditorium Santa Margherita
MAP K5 ■ Campo S Margherita, Dorsoduro 3689

This converted church (see p38) sometimes stages world and other music performances for free. Details are generally posted on the door or online (www.unive.it).

A performance at Teatro Goldoni

10 Teatro Goldoni
MAP P4 ■ Calle del Teatro, S Marco 4650/B ■ Ticket sales: 041 240 20 14 ■ www.teatrostabileveneto.it

Teatro Goldoni is one of the oldest theatres in the city, dating from the 17th century. It acquired its present name in 1875 in honour of the 18th-century playwright Carlo Goldoni (see p52). An excellent range of international plays is performed in Italian between November and May.

TOP 10 FILMS SET IN VENICE

Indiana Jones in Venice

1 Indiana Jones and the Last Crusade (1989)
Hero Harrison Ford heaves up the floor in the church of San Barnaba.

2 Anonimo Veneziano (1970)
This drama, directed by Enrico Maria Salerno, tells the story of a musician who dreams of becoming a conductor.

3 Death in Venice (1971)
Visconti's film starring Dirk Bogarde is now as classic as the Thomas Mann (see p52) novel on which it is based.

4 Don't Look Now (1973)
This thriller, directed by Nicolas Roeg, with Donald Sutherland and Julie Christie, will keep you awake at night.

5 The Merchant of Venice (2004)
Shakespeare adaptation starring Al Pacino as a brilliant Shylock.

6 Senso (1954)
Alida Valli betrays family and country for an Austrian officer in this Visconti film.

7 Fellini's Casanova (1976)
Donald Sutherland walks around a fantasized version of Venice in this Fellini film.

8 The Wings of the Dove (1997)
Helena Bonham Carter stars in the film version of Henry James's Venetian story.

9 Pane e Tulipan (2000)
Soldini's romantic comedy, "Bread and Tulips", follows a woman who hitchhikes to Venice.

10 Dieci Inverni (2009)
In this film by Valerio Mieli, two people fall in love over ten winters.

🔟 Cafés and Gelaterie

① Gelateria Il Doge

A popular ice-cream stop for locals and visitors alike, Gelateria Il Doge (see p101) attracts long queues in the summer. This is partly due to its range of gluten-free ice cream and vegan-friendly *granita* (sorbet), as well as its signature scoop – *Crema del Doge*. The *gelateria* is located in the pretty Campo Santa Margherita square (see p98), which is the perfect place to sit and enjoy your ice cream.

② Bacaro del Gelato

MAP D2 ▪ Fondamenta Misericordia, Cannaregio 2499 ▪ 347 050 77 37

This family-run *gelateria* serves light, artisanal gelato – even the ice lollies only contain fruit. The flavours change frequently, but you can expect to find classic scoops such as chocolate and *tiramisù*, as well as *Crema Veneziana*, which is swirled with orange jam, dark chocolate and praline brittle.

③ Bar Filovia

MAP B3 ▪ Fondamenta S Chiara 521, S Croce ▪ 340 970 67 31

Located under the Ponte della Costituzione, Bar Filovia is the perfect breakfast spot. It is loved by Venetians for its wide selection of croissants, *tramezzini* (sandwiches) and snacks. Classic *tramezzino* fillings include tuna and egg, mozzarella and tomato, and ham and mushroom, but the house speciality is *piccantino* – prosciutto and spicy hot sauce.

Canal-side dining at Gelateria Nico

④ Gelateria Nico

One of the few ice-cream parlours with seating, Gelateria Nico (see p101) is situated right on the waterside, so you can enjoy your gelato, which is served in vintage glassware, while watching the boats float by on the Giudecca Canal. In addition to ice creams, this *gelateria* serves cocktails, making it the perfect spot for refreshment both during the day and in the night.

⑤ Al Todaro

MAP R5 ▪ Piazza S Marco 3, S Marco ▪ 041 528 51 65

This historic ice-cream parlour occupies a magical location in Piazza San Marco (see pp20–21),

Alfresco seating at Al Todaro in Piazza San Marco

overlooking the Grand Canal. The classic gelato flavours served here are reasonably priced.

6 Bar Spritz

MAP M5 ■ Calle dei Frati 30, S Marco 3532/36 ■ 328 595 09 07 ■ Closed Sun

A small bar with a few alfresco tables to enjoy a coffee and a croissant, a light lunch, or an *aperitivo*. The menu has everything from sweet pastries to savoury bruschetta, all at excellent value for money.

7 Suso Gelatoteca

One of the most renowned *gelaterie* in Venice, Suso Gelatoteca *(see p86)* has been serving its rich, homemade ice cream for years. They also offer vegan flavours, which are made with coconut milk and include a water-based dark chocolate scoop. Unlike other Venetian *gelaterie*, the gelato here is served in a crispy wafer cone – rather than a paper cup – so the entire thing is edible and hence, reduces waste.

8 Torrefazione Cannaregio

MAP C1 ■ Fondamenta dei Ormesini, Cannaregio 2804 ■ 041 716 371

Situated close to the Jewish Quarter *(see p103)*, Torrefazione Cannaregio has walls stocked high with jars of different coffee beans. Pick from a variety of blends – from fruity flavours to 100 per cent Arabica – and enjoy a cup in the cafe's brick-and-dark-wood interior. Or, you can buy a paper bag of beans to take home with you. Tea and breakfast pastries are also on offer.

9 La Mela Verde

MAP F4 ■ Fondamenta de l'Osmarin, Castello 4977 ■ 349 195 79 24 ■ Closed Mon & Nov–Mar

This artisan *gelateria* specializes in fruity ice cream and sorbet flavours, complete with pieces of fresh, seasonal fruit. The green apple ice cream, that lends the shop its name, is the highlight. The ricotta and pistachio scoop is highly recommended as well.

10 Nobile Pasticceria

MAP C2 ■ Cannaregio 1818 ■ 041 720 731

This *pâtisserie* is worth visiting at any time of the day. For breakfast, you can order a croissant and the excellent cappuccino, espresso or latte macchiato. At lunchtime, try a *pizzette* (mini pizza) or focaccia and, come evening, enjoy a delicious spritz or cordial. The *pâtisserie*'s traditional Venetian desserts are a must-try too.

Confectionery at Nobile Pasticceria

🔟 Places to Eat in Venice

Alfresco dining at Hotel Cipriani

1 Hotel Cipriani
Guests are ferried from Piazza San Marco to this hotel restaurant (see p127) in a private launch for a memorable gastronomic experience at two venues, Oro and Cip's Club. The former affords stunning views of the lagoon; the latter fantastic vistas of St Mark's Square. *Tagliolini gratinati al prosciutto* (ribbon pasta with ham, browned in the oven) is a speciality.

2 Da Fiore
Reservations are essential at this sophisticated restaurant (see p93), where the owners base the day's menu on what is fresh at the market. They might have *pappardelle con ostriche e zafferano* (flat ribbon pasta with oysters and saffron) or *moleche fritte con polenta* (fried soft-shelled crab with polenta). Excellent use of seasonal produce has made this hidden gem a gourmet heaven.

3 Grand Canal, Hotel Monaco
Set on a terrace overlooking the stunning Grand Canal, this restaurant (see p87) serves traditional Venetian and Italian cuisine of a very high standard, including freshly made pasta with shrimp or delicious seafood risotto, accompanied by the best of European wines.

4 Ostaria Boccadoro
Romantically situated beneath a vine-clad pergola, the charming Ostaria Boccadoro (see p107) offers creative dishes with delicate flavours and fresh ingredients, such as ribbon pasta with scallops and courgette (zucchini) flowers. Beware the superb *mousse al cioccolato* – it's made with five different kinds of chocolate!

5 Corte Sconta
This former *osteria* is now a trendy restaurant (see p113) that serves memorable seafood in a pretty "hidden courtyard" (*corte sconta*). Don't miss the *pincia*, the local bread pudding, for dessert. The house wine is also wonderful. Booking several days in advance is essential for most of the year.

6 Do Forni
Customers enter an imitation Orient Express dining car to be greeted by displays of glistening seafood at this award-winning restaurant (see p87) popular with business people, located right by Piazza San Marco. Book ahead.

7 Vini da Gigio
The owner prides himself on his Italian and foreign wines to accompany dishes such as *tagliata*

di tonno (fresh tuna fillet with herbs) and agnello (lamb) at this tiny well-established restaurant *(see p107)* with a great reputation. Booking is recommended.

8 La Bitta
The cosy, rustic La Bitta *(see p101)* specializes in succulent meat dishes served with seasonal vegetables and superb wines. The innovative menu changes almost every day according to market availability and never includes fish.

9 Osteria Santa Marina
Seafood is the star of the menu at this elegant restaurant *(see p113)*; the baby octopus with red onion and orange is highly recommended. There is a wonderful six-course tasting menu of Venetian specialities. The wine list is impressive too.

10 Trattoria alla Madonna
This popular restaurant *(see p87)* is the perfect place for traditional dishes such as delicate *granseola* (spider crab). An inspiring display of fresh seafood, such as *spaghetti con nero* (with cuttlefish ink sauce) and *anguilla fritta* (fried eel), is available here as well. It is not possible to make a reservation, so expect to queue.

Trattoria alla Madonna

TOP 10 VENETIAN DISHES

Tiramisù, a classic Italian dessert

1 Tiramisù
Dessert with a creamy sauce of eggs and mascarpone between layers of sponge drenched in coffee or liqueur.

2 Carpaccio
Raw beef sliced thin and sprinkled with rocket *(rucola)* or flakes of Parmesan cheese.

3 Sarde in Saor
Fried sardines marinated in a sweet-and-sour mixture of onions, currants and pine nuts, invented for sailors at sea for lengthy periods.

4 Antipasto di Frutti di Mare
Seafood platter of baby octopus, anchovies, shrimp or whatever else is in season.

5 Prosciutto e Melone
The sweetness of wedges of fresh rock melon is contrasted with the slightly salty cured Parma ham.

6 Risotto di Pesce
Clams, mussels, shrimp and assorted fish in a heavenly creamy rice dish.

7 Pasta con il Nero di Seppia
Usually spaghetti, combined with a rich sauce of tomato and cuttlefish, thoroughly blackened with the ink.

8 Fegato alla Veneziana
Venetian-style calves' liver cooked slowly with onions and vinegar.

9 Grilled Fish
Such as *coda di rospo* (monkfish) or *pesce spada* (swordfish) from the south.

10 Grilled Vegetables
Radicchio (red chicory) in winter, *zucchine* (courgettes) and *melanzane* (aubergine/eggplant) in summer, and roasted *peperoni* (peppers).

🔟 Osterie (Wine Bars)

Polenta pots and wine behind the bar at Cantina Do Mori

1 Cantina Do Mori
MAP N2 ■ Calle dei Do Mori, S Polo 429 ■ Closed Sun

Rows of copper polenta pots hang overhead in this dark, popular bar, billed as the city's oldest *osteria*. The affable owners pour wine directly from huge demijohns and serve delicate postage-stamp-sized ham and salad sandwiches *(francobolli)*.

2 Un Mondo diVino
MAP E3 ■ Salizzada S Canciano, Cannaregio 5984A ■ Closed Thu

Italian wines can be enjoyed at this converted butcher's shop, along with mouthwatering bar snacks such as *insalata di mare* (seafood salad) and regional cheeses. This place is well frequented by both locals and visitors, who spill out from the bar and into the alleyway, glass in hand.

3 Osteria Ruga Rialto
MAP N3 ■ Ruga Vecchia S Giovanni, S Polo 692A ■ Closed Thu

Verging on rowdy, this traditional establishment turns out crisp fried calamari and vegetables at evening *aperitivo* time, when you'll have to elbow your way past the locals to reach the bar. Lunch and dinner are somewhat quieter affairs.

4 Osteria del Sacro e Profano
MAP P2 ■ Ramo secondo del Parangon, S Polo 502 ■ Closed Sun dinner

Well worth hunting out near Rialto, this rustic-looking *osteria* is the haunt of international artists, who happily mingle with the locals. Wines from the Veneto and Friuli are served with traditional snacks such as *uova con acciughe* (hard-boiled egg with anchovy).

5 Enoteca do Colonne
MAP C2 ■ Rio Terrà del Cristo, Cannaregio 1814C

All manner of counter food *(cicchetti)*, ranging from *baccalà* (salted cod) on crusty bread to hearty *musetto* sausage, is served with great smiles

Food counter at Enoteca do Colonne

by the affable young owners at this lively neighbourhood bar. There's a also a good selection of Veneto wines.

6 Estro
MAP K4 ■ Calle San Pantalon, Dorsoduro 3778 ■ Closed Tue

Run by two Venetian brothers, this stylish *enoteca* serves a fantastic range of wines from all over the world, along with dishes made from locally grown, seasonal ingredients.

7 Osteria alla Frasca
MAP E2 ■ Corte della Carità, Cannaregio 5176

Said to be the site where Titian kept his paints and canvases, this is now a tiny picturesque bar serving drinks and snacks on a vine-covered terrace in summer.

8 Trattoria Antico Calice
MAP Q3 ■ Calle dei Stagneri, S Marco 5228

You have to fight your way through the locals here, attracted by the lively atmosphere and counter overflowing with local wines and appetizing snacks such as fried sardines in breadcrumbs.

9 Trattoria Ca' d'Oro alla Vedova
MAP D2 ■ Calle del Pistor, Cannaregio 3912 ■ Open Fri–Wed

A young and enterprising team runs this timber-panelled venue, which has been serving mouthwatering *cicchetti*, such as crispy battered artichokes and meatballs *(polpette)*, along with quaffable wine, for longer than any of the regulars can remember. There are also main dishes, served at tables.

10 Cantine del Vino già Schiavi
MAP C5 ■ Fondamenta Nani, Dorsoduro 992 ■ Closed Sun

Join the locals at this family-run specialist wine cellar, located near the Accademia Bridge, for excellent prosecco at the stand-up bar. Simple nibbles to accompany the wine include *mortadella* sausage and *panini* filled with *sopressa*, a local salami.

TOP 10 BEVERAGES

Refreshing Spritz al Bitter

1 Spritz
Venetian favourite of white wine with a splash of Bitter, Aperol or Select *(aperitivo* brands) and a shot of mineral water.

2 Prosecco
Excellent, sparkling, dry white wine from the hills around Conegliano and Valdobbiadene.

3 Bellini
Smooth fresh peach juice and sparkling prosecco blend, invented by Cipriani of Harry's Bar *(see p25)* located at Calle Vallaresso, S Marco 1323.

4 Red Wine
An *ombra* means a small glass of house wine, otherwise try quality Cabernet, Valpolicella or Amarone.

5 White Wine
Soave and Pinot Grigio are worthwhile alternatives to house varieties.

6 Mineral Water
Widely served in Italy, either sparkling *(gasata)* or still *(naturale)*. Tap water is *acqua dal rubinetto*.

7 Fruit Drinks
These can be ordered as *spremuta* (freshly squeezed juice) or *succo di frutta* (bottled nectars).

8 Coffee
Straight espresso, frothy cappuccino or *caffè latte* in a tall glass with hot milk.

9 Hot Chocolate
Usually served in the winter months. An *espresso* milk-free version can be found in good chocolate emporia.

10 Sgroppino
Made with lemon sorbet, vodka and prosecco, and served between courses.

🔟 Shops in Venice

1 Ca' Macana

Buy one of Venice's famous papier-mâché masks at this shop (see p63), which carries the full Carnival range and much more besides. You can watch the mask-makers in action or even attend a course in making or painting your own masks using feathers, rhine-stones, trimmings or glitter.

2 Nardi

MAP Q5 ■ Piazza S Marco 69, S Marco

Elizabeth Taylor, Grace Kelly and Elton John have all happily spent time (and more) in this plush bou-tique of glittering marvels. Three generations of crafters have thrilled those who can afford it with breath-taking pieces, such as rings with Venetian masks or gold bracelets with amber, turquoise and diamonds.

3 Luigi Bevilacqua

MAP L2 ■ Campiello della Comare, S Croce 1320 ■ Closed Sun

Shimmering velvets, silks and damasks are fashioned into wonderful bags, clothes and shoes. The Bevilacqua family has been weaving precious fab-rics by hand since the 1700s and you can see the ancient looms they continue to use today.

Colourful façade of Venini

4 Venini

MAP Q4 ■ Piazzetta Leoncini, S Marco 314

You may not find Venetian glass animals here, however you can admire innovative platters and vases of simplicity and style. Since its 1921 beginnings, Venini's award-winning design team has included top names Carlo Scarpa and Gae Aulenti.

5 Attombri

MAP P3 ■ Sottoportico degli Orefici, S Polo 65

Beautifully crafted bead jewellery is made on the premises by bro-thers Stefano and Daniele. Pieces range from delicate earrings to flamboyant necklaces.

6 Rizzo

MAP Q2 ■ Salizada S Giovanni Crisostomo, Cannaregio 5778 ■ Open Mon–Sat

Jet-black tagliatelle ribbons coloured with cuttlefish ink are just one option out of more than 40 imaginative pasta shapes that can be found on sale at Rizzo. Handmade chocolates and multicoloured Carnival masks also make marvellous souvenirs to take home.

7 T Fondaco dei Tedeschi

MAP P3 ■ Calle del Fontego dei Tedeschi, Rialto Bridge, 30124

Originally used as a warehouse and lodgings for German traders,

Ancient looms at Luigi Bevilacqua

this old building has now been completely refurbished as a popular luxury department store. The lovely rooftop terrace is known for its stunning views.

8 Rubelli
MAP M4 ■ Campiello del Teatro, S Marco 3877 ■ Open Mon–Sat

Venice's past contact with the Orient is conjured up by the sumptuous handmade furnishings in this showroom. A blend of computer technology and traditional techniques is used for the brocades, damasks and silks.

Wide range of paper at Paolo Olbi

9 Paolo Olbi
MAP N4 ■ Dorsoduro 3253/A

This shop contains exquisite photo albums and address books in rainbow-coloured marbled paper and leather. All at reasonable prices, they are made by one of the original crafters in Venice.

10 Signor Blum
The meticulously hand-crafted and hand-painted wooden items on display in this corner store *(see p100)*, make for original presents and souvenirs. The range includes pictures of the city's landmark buildings and portraits of outstanding musicians as fridge magnets.

TOP 10 SOUVENIRS

Murano glassware

1 Glassware
Impress your guests back home with a genuine Murano chandelier or perhaps a *millefiori* paperweight.

2 Gourmet Food
For something typicaly Italian but intrinsically Venetian, try extra virgin olive oil flavoured with chilli peppers, bottled red chicory paste or pasta in the shape of gondolas and masks.

3 T-shirts
The essential guaranteed souvenir of Venice, sold at the ubiquitous street stalls.

4 Masks
A mind-boggling array of masks, traditionally made for Carnival in papier-mâché, ceramic and even leather.

5 Marbled Paper
Swirls of pastel hues can be used for covering books or simply as elegant wrapping paper for gifts.

6 Beads
All manner of beads, from frosted glass to ceramic or the traditional, colourful murrhine mosaic-style, can be found.

7 Italian Wine and Liqueurs
Take advantage of lower prices and taxes by stocking up on locally produced wines.

8 Fabric
Lace is the most Venetian of materials, but attractive linens and velvets are also good value.

9 Silverwork
Photo frames, letter openers and teaspoons make lovely gifts for friends.

10 Clothes
All the top fashion names can be found in Venice.

🔟 Venice for Free

Mosaics in the Basilica di San Marco

1 Basilica di San Marco

Entry to the city's main church (see pp12–13), plastered with glittering Byzantine mosaics, is free of charge. Modelled on Saint Sophia in Constantinople, the basilica is a glorious reflection of the city's Byzantine connection. The cavernous building has walls lined with artistically cut rock-slabs and superb geometric patterns on the floor.

2 Take a Free Walking Tour

www.venicefreewalkingtour.com

Every morning and afternoon, free guided walking tours in English are organized from Campo Santi Apostoli in Cannaregio. Knowledgeable volunteers accompany visitors on short walks through places off the beaten track. It is essential to book ahead to ensure a place.

3 Art Night

www.artnightvenezia.it

Concerts, exhibitions, lectures, demonstrations of craft techniques, and videos are on all over the city on a set night in June (see the website), all organized by the City Council and Ca' Foscari University. Reservations are necessary for some events.

4 Free Museum Entry

On the first Sunday of each month, entry to all Italian state-run museums and galleries is free for all visitors. In Venice, this includes the Gallerie dell'Accademia, Galleria Franchetti alla Ca' d'Oro, Museo Archeologico, Museo d'Arte Orientale and Palazzo Grimani.

5 Watching the Boats Go By

Settle down on any canal edge, and enjoy the unique sight of people going about their day-to-day business by boat – rubbish barges, transport floats, florist boats, taxi launches, to mention a few. And the water is often shared by ducks and cormorants fishing. Choice spots are Punta della Dogana (see p98), the Zattere (see p97) and the main Cannaregio canal.

6 T Fondaco dei Tedeschi Rooftop Terrace

MAP P3 ▪ Calle del Fontego dei Tedeschi, Rialto Bridge, S Marco ▪ 041 314 20 00 ▪ Open daily (times vary) ▪ www.dfs.com

Located at the foot of the Rialto Bridge, this modern department store is housed in the former main post office building, which has been transformed into luxury shops. The top of the building affords spectacular views – book a free visit online.

7 Museo della Musica

MAP N6 ▪ Chiesa di S Maurizio, Campo S Maurizio, S Marco ▪ 041 241 18 40 ▪ www.museodellamusica.com

This fascinating museum in converted church premises offers free entrance, allowing visitors to admire its historical collection of remarkable musical instruments dating back to the time of Vivaldi.

Museo della Musica

8 Isola di San Michele Cemetery

An island circled by tall brick walls and dotted with cypress trees houses the city's monumental cemetery *(see p118)*. Even if you have little interest in paying homage at the tombs of notable residents Igor Stravinsky, Diaghilev or Joseph Brodsky, it's a pleasant spot simply for strolling around.

Isola di San Michele Cemetery

9 Castello Giardini Pubblici

Over in the Castello district, these gardens *(see p111)* were laid out in the late 1800s by the French occupiers, as quickly becomes clear from the style. Shade and benches can be enjoyed to rest your weary feet, while the children let off steam in the playground.

Castello Giardini Pubblici

10 Free Concerts

In neighbourhood halls and churches, orchestras and choirs from Italy and overseas often hold concerts, which are free to spectators. To find out about these events in advance, check the street posters affixed to the city walls.

TOP 10 BUDGET TIPS

Avoiding café service charges

1 To avoid the waiter service charge at cafés, do as the locals do and take your drink at the bar instead of sitting down at a table.

2 For cheap accommodation search for last-minute deals online.

3 A house exchange is a low-cost way to experience Venice – and to live as the locals do.

4 Admire masterpieces – paintings and sculptures – in the city's multiple churches, where admission charges are modest.

5 Buy a slice of pizza at one of the many *pizza al taglio* establishments. It's the perfect food option when you're on the go.

6 Buy picnic supplies at a supermarket, and fill up your water bottle at a tap or fountain. For picnic areas see #EnjoyRespectVenezia at www.comune.venezia.it

7 Purchase a Venezia Unica pass in advance online *(www.veneziaunica.it)*. You can use this for ferries and sightseeing, saving both queuing time and money.

8 During the Biennale art event every two years *(www.labiennale.org)*, visit the many free shows that are dotted around the city.

9 Cheap fashion clothes and shoes are on sale at the weekly markets on the Lido on Tuesday.

10 The Rolling Venice card *(www.veneziaunica.it)* offers discounted rates at shops and restaurants for young visitors (those aged 6–29).

🔟 Festivals and Events

1 Carnival
Feb–Mar, concluding on Shrove Tue, 40 days before Easter

This 10-day extravaganza takes over the city as a countdown to Lent. The

streets mill with costumed and masked local "nobility" and visitors. It starts with the Volo dell'Angelo (flight of the angel), when either an acrobat or a cardboard dove is launched from the Campanile in Piazza San Marco, showering onlookers with confetti. The grand finale is the explosive Mardi Gras.

Carnival-goer in full costume

2 Su e Zo per i Ponti
Late Mar/Apr: 4th Sun in Lent
■ www.suezo.it

Anyone can join this non-competitive walk or run "up and down the bridges". Some official routes include an 11-km (6.5-miles) route that runs over 39 bridges and a 5-km route (3-miles) that runs over 18 bridges. All participants receive a medal on finishing.

3 Festa della Sensa
May: Ascension Day

Head for the Riviera di San Nicolò at the Lido (see p123) to watch this ancient ceremony of "Venice wedding to the Sea". A costumed "doge" casts a ring into the sea amid a procession of celebratory boats. Symbolizing Venice's maritime supremacy, La Sensa has been staged since Venice took Istria and Dalmatia in AD 997.

4 Vogalonga
May: Sun after Ascension

A colourful armada of rowing craft from all over the world embarks on a 32-km (20-mile) non-competitive route around the lagoon's scattered islands. The "Long Row" is a great experience for both participants and onlookers, who line the Canale di Cannaregio towards midday to cheer on the breathtaking final stretch down the Grand Canal.

5 Biennale Art Exhibition
Jun–Nov ■ www.labiennale.org

The world's leading international art bonanza is held on a two-yearly basis. The leafy gardens in eastern Castello are the principal venue, supplemented by the Corderie building in the Arsenale.

6 Festa del Redentore
Mid-Jul: Sat pm

People crowd on to all available watercraft, decorated with paper lanterns and greenery, for a feast of roast duck and watermelon, followed by a midnight fireworks display. It all takes place near Palladio's church on

Midnight fireworks on Festa del Redentore

Giudecca *(see p123)* to commemorate the end of the 1576 plague. For those getting there on foot, a temporary pontoon bridge stretches from the Zattere over the Giudecca canal.

Festa di San Rocco
16 Aug

The feast day of St Roch, the French saint adopted by the confraternity for alleviating the 1576–7 plague, is celebrated each year at the Scuola Grande di San Rocco *(see p89)*.

Colourful boats at Regata Storica

Regata Storica
1st Sun in Sep

The word regatta originated in Venice At the year's most spectacular event, ornately decorated boats propelled by costumed oarsmen parade down the Grand Canal with passengers dressed as historical dignitaries. A series of furiously contested regattas follows.

Venice Marathon
Late Oct

Runners from all parts of the globe begin this classic – not to mention beautiful – 42-km (26-mile) race at Villa Pisani on the Brenta waterway, cross the causeway to Venice, the Zattere and San Marco, and finish near the public gardens in Castello. Other race routes are 21 km (13 miles) and 10 km (6.5 miles) long.

Festa della Salute
21 Nov

Venetians make a pilgrimage to Longhena's church *(see p48)* every winter in memory of the devastating plague of 1630–31. The whole area assumes a festive atmosphere with stalls selling candy floss and balloons.

TOP 10 SPORTS IN VENICE

A women's rowing team practising

1 Rowing
MAP D5 ▪ Zattere, Dorsoduro
Immensely popular Venetian pastime practised standing up. Join the oldest club, Canottieri Bucintoro.

2 Cycling
MAP H2 ▪ Gran Viale SM Elisabetta
Illegal in Venice itself, though you'll see kids zooming around. It is allowed in Lido, where you can rent a bike from a cycle shop on the main street.

3 Sailing
Yachtsmen gather at the marina on San Giorgio Maggiore island.

4 Swimming
Head for the Lido, or the crowded indoor pools at Sacca Fisola and Sant'Alvise.

5 In-Line Skating
There is a small rink at Sant'Elena in Castello, otherwise stick to the Lido *(see p123)* pavements.

6 Golf
MAP H2 ▪ Strada Vecchia, 1
The well-reputed 18-hole course at the Alberoni is on the south of the Lido.

7 Tennis
MAP H2 ▪ Lungomare G Marconi 41/D
The Lido has the only courts available to visitors.

8 Jogging
The city's stone paving doesn't do wonders for your knees, so try the city parks.

9 Gyms
Private gyms with state-of-the-art equipment, located in the city, can be found online.

10 Football
MAP H2 ▪ Stadio Pierluigi Penzo
The home team Venezia plays at Sant'Elena stadium on Sundays.

Venice
Area by Area

Lungo and Rio di San
Trovaso, Dorsoduro

🔟 San Marco

Venice's smallest but foremost *sestiere* (district), named after the city's patron saint, is bounded by the Grand Canal on all but one side, which explains the number of stately palaces in the area. It revolves around Piazza San Marco and the majestic Doge's Palace, the political and legal core of the city until the 18th century. Running off the square are the Mercerie and Calle Larga XXII Marzo, offering wall-to-wall designer shopping. But beyond that San Marco has a residential air, with a great range of places to eat. Don't hesitate to wander down minor alleyways: surprises include unusual wellheads and many craft workshops.

Niccolò Tommaseo

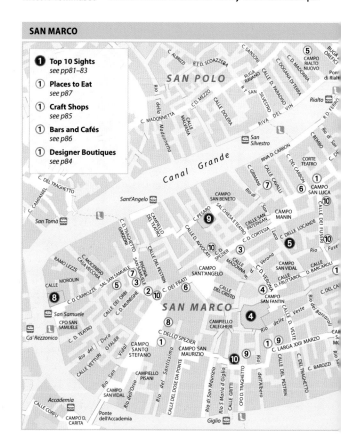

SAN MARCO

- **1** Top 10 Sights
  see pp81–83
- **1** Places to Eat
  see p87
- **1** Craft Shops
  see p85
- **1** Bars and Cafés
  see p86
- **1** Designer Boutiques
  see p84

1 Piazza San Marco
See pp20–23.

2 Mercerie
MAP Q4

The expensive elegance of Venice is most evident on this main thoroughfare linking Rialto and Piazza San Marco. *Mercerie* means "haberdasher's", but these days it is home to designer fashion outlets. Just below the ornate Torre dell'Orologio archway is a sculpted female figure commemorating a housewife who lived here rent-free as a reward for inadvertently knocking a mortar into the street, killing a revolutionary leader and so halting the short-lived Bajamonte Tiepolo revolt in 1310.

3 Basilica di San Marco

Built on a Greek cross plan, and crowned with five huge domes, this is the third church *(see pp12–15)* to stand on this site. In 1807, it succeeded San Pietro in Castello as the cathedral of Venice. Dark, mysterious and enriched with the spoils of conquest, the basilica is a unique blend of Eastern and Western influences. Embellished over a period of six centuries, it features fabulous mosaics, marble and carvings and served as a fitting location for ceremonies of the Republic. It was here that the elected doge was presented to the city following his election. This is also where sea captains came to pray for protection before embarking on epic voyages.

4 Teatro La Fenice
MAP N5 ■ Campo S Fantin
■ Open daily for guided tours

Long masked in scaffolding since a 1996 arson attack left it gutted, the historic "Phoenix" theatre rose from the flames in 2003. Selva's 1792 opera house has staged countless world premieres including Rossini's *Tancredi* in 1813, five operas commissioned of Verdi, most notably *Rigoletto* and *La Traviata*, and works by Stravinsky and Luigi Nono. Legendary divas such as Maria Callas and Dame Joan Sutherland have sung in this glorious setting *(see p64)*.

Concert at Teatro La Fenice

⑤ Scala Contarini del Bovolo

MAP P4 ▪ Corte dei Risi, S Marco 4303 ▪ Open Nov–Feb: 9:30am–5:30pm (last admission 5pm); Mar–Oct: 10am–6pm (last admission 5:30pm) daily ▪ Adm ▪ www.gioiellinascostidivenezia.it

Often used as a film set, this fine 15th-century palace with its beautiful external "snail-shell" staircase (*bovolo* means snail in Venetian) is squeezed into a diminutive square deep in San Marco. Visitors can climb the winding steps of the staircase, a blend of Renaissance, Gothic and Byzantine styles, via five floors of loggias to a dome sheltering a splendid belvedere. From here there are magical panoramic views over the city's rooftops.

GLASSMAKING

Venetian glasswork exquisitely decorates chandeliers, chalices and mirrors and has long been in demand the world over, especially during the 16th century. Although the industry moved to Murano (**above**) in 1295 as a safety measure against fire, there are still many furnaces around the San Marco district that welcome visitors.

⑥ Campo San Bartolomeo

MAP P3 ▪ Chiesa di San Bartolomeo: open 10am–noon Tue, Thu & Sat

The statue of celebrated Venetian playwright Carlo Goldoni scrutinizes the milling crowds on this crossroads square. Strategically placed for a host of inviting bars crammed into the alleys radiating off it, "San Bartolo" is a hang-out spot for the city's young and trendy. The northern end is occupied by the main post office, once home to Venice's German community (see p51). They worshipped in the Chiesa di San Bartolomeo.

Carlo Goldoni

⑦ Doge's Palace

The seat of the Venetian government from the 9th century until the fall of the Republic in 1797, the Doge's Palace (see pp16–19) was the official residence of the Venetian ruler, known as the doge. It started life as a fortified castle in the 9th century, but this and several subsequent buildings were destroyed by a series of fires. A Gothic masterpiece, the bulk of the pink marble building appears perched on loggias and arcades of white Istrian stone.

Allegorical historical paintings embellish the walls and ceilings of the halls and chambers. These rooms are testament to the glory of the Venetian Republic.

⑧ Palazzo Grassi

MAP L5 ▪ Campo S Samuele, S Marco 3231 ▪ Open 10am–7pm Wed–Mon (last admission 6pm) ▪ Adm (includes Punta della Dogana) ▪ www.palazzograssi.it

Set on the Grand Canal, Palazzo Grassi (see p56) dates back to 1740, when a wealthy merchant family commissioned Giorgio Massari to design the building. It is now home to the François Pinault collection, housing contemporary masterpieces by Jeff Koons, Damien Hirst and Michelangelo Pistoletto. It stands alongside picturesque Campo San Samuele, which features a graceful Veneto-Byzantine bell tower.

⑨ Museo Fortuny

MAP N4 ▪ Campo S Benedetto, S Marco 3780 ▪ Open 10am–5pm Wed–Mon (last admission 4pm) ▪ Adm ▪ www.visitmuve.it

Flamboyant Spanish artist and theatrical stage designer Mariano Fortuny y Madrazo (1871–1950) adopted Venice as his home and muse, and transformed this 15th-century palace in Gothic-Venetian style into an atelier. The building retains rooms created by Fortuny himself and visitors can admire Fortuny's gorgeous velvets, his famous pleated silk dresses, some 150 paintings, lamps, a remarkable stage curtain and fascinating 19th-century photographs. The museum also hosts temporary exhibitions.

Exhibits at Museo Fortuny

⑩ Chiesa di Santa Maria del Giglio

MAP N6 ■ Campo S Maria del Giglio, S Marco 3231 ■ Open 10:30am–1:30pm & 2:30–5pm Mon–Sat ■ Adm ■ www.chorusvenezia.org

Opening on to a lovely square next to the Grand Canal, this church is a further example of Venetian Baroque extravagance. Commissioned by the Barbaro family, its façade exalts their generations of maritime and political triumphs, with crests, galleys and statues. Works of art inside the church include Venice's only canvas by Rubens, depicting a Madonna and child. Tintoretto's contributions are the Evangelists on the organ doors.

Ceiling fresco in the Chiesa di Santa Maria del Giglio

A DAY IN SAN MARCO

▶ MORNING

Visit the **Doge's Palace** *(see pp16–19)* on **Piazza San Marco** *(see pp20–23)*. Must-sees at the palace include the Sala del Senato, Sala del Maggior Consiglio, prisons and the Bridge of Sighs. Then take a break for coffee in the modern café in the palace's former stables and watch the gondolas glide past the glassed-in doorway.

Time your visit to **Basilica di San Marco** *(see p81)* for midday, to catch the mosaics illuminated by huge spotlights so they glitter to their utmost. The tiles were laid at angles to catch the light.

Have lunch at **Harry's Bar** *(see p25)*, as Hemingway's hero did in *Across the River and into the Trees*. Order the *carpaccio* (wafer-thin slices of raw beef) invented here by Cipriani *(see p25)*.

AFTERNOON

The **Mercerie** *(see p81)* is shopper's heaven, packed with international high-fashion stores from Benetton to Cartier, and classy souvenir glass and hand-crafted paper workshops. For yet more, cross over to Calle Larga XXII Marzo for designer delights such as **Bulgari** *(see p84)* and **Cartier** jewellery *(see p84)*.

Return to **Piazza San Marco** *(see pp20–23)* in time to enjoy the views over Venice and the lagoon from the Campanile at dusk. Watch the sun set behind the basilica, while enjoying a Bellini *aperitivo* at **Caffè Florian** *(see pp20–21)*.

See map on pp80–81

Designer Boutiques

① Frette
MAP P5 ■ Frezzeria,
S Marco 1725

Since 1860, Frette has been importing top-grade cotton from Egypt and transforming it into towels and custom-made household linen.

Interior of L'Isola – Carlo Moretti

② L'Isola – Carlo Moretti
MAP M5 ■ Calle delle
Botteghe, S Marco 2970

Exhibited in galleries all over the world, this is contemporary glass at its most innovative. Moretti's trademarks are "paper cone" vases, tumblers and huge sculptures.

③ Le Perle
MAP D3 ■ Ponte di Rialto,
S Marco 5329

Murano glass and jewellery come together in this workshop on the Rialto Bridge, resulting in brightly coloured, but elegant, pieces.

④ Ottico Urbani
MAP E4 ■ San Marco
Frezzeria, S Marco 1280

The Urbani brothers have been designing eyewear since 1953, creating frames from unique materials such as fabric and wood. Their designs are a favourite with celebrities visiting the city for the International Film Festival.

⑤ Cartier
MAP P5 ■ Calle San Moisè,
S Marco 1474

The fortress-like premises of these world-famous French jewellers gleam with gold, precious stones and well-crafted handbags and watches.

⑥ MaxMara
MAP P3 ■ Campo S Salvador,
S Marco 5033

This family company has been designing fashionable clothes and accessories for city girls since 1951.

⑦ Bulgari
MAP P5 ■ Salizzada San Moisè,
S Marco 1494

Striking contemporary jewellery, watches, accessories and Rosenthal porcelain are sold here.

⑧ Fratelli Rossetti
MAP P3 ■ Campo S Salvador,
S Marco 4800

This family-run firm was established in 1953 and is known worldwide for the superb Italian elegance it displays in the likes of shoes, belts, bags and jackets.

⑨ Fendi
MAP P5 ■ Frezzeria,
S Marco 1225

Go straight to the source for flamboyant frocks and shoes for special occasions and crazily beaded bags, all sporting the "double-F" Fendi mark.

⑩ Arnoldo e Battois
MAP P4 ■ Calle dei Fuseri,
S Marco 4271

Fabulous Italian fashion is available here from designers Silvano Arnoldo and Massimiliano Battois – let them help you create your look in this minimalist cube of a store.

**Arnoldo e Battois
shoulder bag**

Craft Shops

1 Venetia Studium
MAP P5 ■ Calle Larga XXII Marzo, S Marco 2425

Exquisite hanging silk lamps of Fortuny design are reproduced with hand-painted patterning and glass beading.

2 I Muschieri
MAP P5 ■ Calle Frezzaria, S Marco 1178

A must for perfume lovers, this small shop is run by two famous Venetian sisters, who create bespoke fragrances for customers.

3 BAC Art Studio
MAP M5 ■ Calle delle Botteghe, S Marco 3451

This art gallery sells attractive and affordable etchings and prints of Venice by artists Baruffaldi and Cadore.

4 Max Art
MAP P5 ■ Frezzeria, S Marco 1232

Commedia dell'arte marionettes, musical puppet theatres and glittering Carnival masks are available here for sale or hire.

5 Caigo Da Mar
MAP M5 ■ Salizada San Samuele, S Marco 3157/A

A speciality boutique, Caigo Da Mar offers luxurious home decor items and jewellery.

6 Rigattieri
MAP M5 ■ Calle dei Frati, S Marco 3532/36

Ceramics enthusiasts must not miss this extraordinary shop of beautiful pottery. It has been run by the same family since it was founded – at this address – in 1938, and the focus is firmly on high-quality pieces.

Venetia Studium copper-leaf free-standing lamp

7 Valese Fonditore
MAP Q4 ■ Calle Fiubera, S Marco 793

The Valese family foundry has been creating their animals, lamps and door knockers in brass and bronze since 1913. Examples of their work can even be found in Buckingham Palace and The White House.

8 Le Botteghe della Solidarietà
MAP P3 ■ Salizzada Pio X, S Marco 5164

A kaleidoscopic display of handwoven shawls from India and musical instruments from African countries are part of an enterprise that is intended to guarantee artisans a just income.

9 Bevilacqua
MAP N5 ■ Campo S Maria del Giglio, S Marco 2520

Handmade velvet and silk cushions and tapestries are a feast for the eyes at this small branch of the historic Italian fabric shop *(see p72)*.

Bevilacqua fabric shop

10 Daniela Ghezzo Segalin a Venezia
MAP P4 ■ Calle dei Fuseri, S Marco 4365

In addition to the brocade slippers and bizarre footwear with built-in toes, special-order shoes are also hand-crafted here.

See map on pp80–81

Bars and Cafés

① Pasticceria Marchini Time
MAP P4 ■ Campo S Luca, S Marco 4589

A paradise for those with a sweet tooth, Marchini is one of the oldest *pasticcerie* in the city. Orange and pistachio chocolates come in Venetian mask shapes.

② I Rusteghi
MAP Q3 ■ Corte del Tintor, S Marco 5513

Tucked away behind Campo San Bartolomeo, this is a cosy *osteria* run by a friendly sommelier-owner. It has an excellent selection of wines and *cicchetti* (bar snacks).

③ Caffè Brasilia
MAP N4 ■ Rio Terrà Assassini, S Marco 3658

Tuck into a huge, fresh fruit salad smothered with yogurt or a *tramezzino* (sandwich) in this quiet side-alley café, with tables inside and a few outside. The coffee's good, too.

④ Bar al Theatro
MAP N5 ■ Campo S Fantin, S Marco 1916

Next door to the renowned Teatro la Fenice *(see p81)*, this legendary venue offers outdoor seating on a patio. Alternatively, go inside to the bar and munch a toasted sandwich.

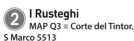

Lime cocktail at Bacarando

⑤ Suso Gelatoteca
MAP Q3 ■ Sotoportego de la Bissa 5453 ■ 041 241 22 75

Try the peanut ice cream at this gorgeous *gelateria (see p67)*. Expect silky, smooth scoops and delicious vegan options. It's expensive, but worth it.

⑥ Bacarando
MAP P3 ■ Corte dell'Orso, S Marco 5495

This great spot offers bar snacks at *aperitivo* time, but also has an elegant restaurant. Wednesday nights see the addition of live music.

⑦ Enoteca Al Volto
MAP D4 ■ Calle Cavalli, San Marco 4081

Located near the town hall, this cosy and traditional *osteria* serves mouth-watering snacks such as the Venetian *cicchetti*. Popular with the locals, it fills up quickly on weekdays.

⑧ Le Café
MAP M5 ■ Campo S Stefano, S Marco 2797

Have a fresh orange juice or cappuccino and pastry as you watch life go by in the square. The usual hot dishes are available, and there is also a *pasticceria* offering tasty tarts and pastries.

⑨ Rosa Salva
MAP Q4 ■ Ponte Ferai, S Marco 950

Come here to enjoy fruit tarts that melt in the mouth, exquisite pastries and Venice's best panettone.

⑩ Bar all'Angolo
MAP M5 ■ Campo Santo Stefano, S Marco 3464 ■ Closed Sun

Tourists and locals alike are unable to resist this great sandwich bar. Bag a table outside for a well-earned coffee or light lunch.

Diners at the Bar al Theatro

Places to Eat

PRICE CATEGORIES

For a three-course meal for one with half a bottle of wine (or equivalent meal), taxes and extra charges.

€ under €40 ■ €€ €40–60 ■ €€€ over €60

1 Ristorante A Beccafico

MAP M5 ■ Campo S Stefano, S Marco 2801 ■ 041 527 48 79 ■ €€€

The menu at this restaurant blends Sicilian dishes with Venetian cuisine and includes pasta, meat and fish, plus fabulous desserts.

2 Grand Canal

MAP Q6 ■ Calle Vallaresso, S Marco 1332 ■ 041 520 02 11 ■ €€€

Part of Hotel Monaco, Grand Canal (see p68) offers stylish dining all year round. The extensive menu features Venetian cuisine and fish dishes.

3 Do Forni

MAP Q4 ■ Calle Specchieri, S Marco, 468 ■ 041 523 21 48 ■ €€€

This elegant restaurant (see p68) has a long list of celebrity guests. The menu features seasonal specialities and an extensive wine list.

4 Rosticceria San Bartolomeo

MAP P3 ■ Calle della Bissa, S Marco 5424 ■ 041 522 35 69 ■ €

Also known as the Gislon, this place serves great mozzarella in carozza, a deep-fried cheese sandwich.

5 Trattoria alla Madonna

MAP P3 ■ Calle della Madonna, S Polo 594 ■ 041 522 38 24 ■ Closed Wed, 25 Dec–31 Jan ■ €€

A well-known, bustling restaurant (see p69), perfect for traditional seafood. Seafood risotto is a speciality.

6 Osteria Leon Bianco

MAP P4 ■ Campo S Luca, S Marco 4153 ■ 041 522 11 80 ■ €

This spot is a great choice for grilled meats and fish or a plate of lasagne. You have the choice of eating at the bar or at a table outside. American Express is not accepted.

7 Al Bacareto

MAP M5 ■ Calle delle Botteghe, S Marco 3447 ■ 041 528 93 36 ■ Closed Sun, Aug ■ €

A Venetian stalwart since 1971, Al Bacareto serves typical local dishes. Try the bigoli in salsa (spaghetti with anchovy and onion purée).

8 Osteria Enoteca San Marco

MAP P5 ■ Frezzeria, S Marco 1610 ■ 041 528 52 42 ■ €€

An exemplary wine list accompanies the tasty bar snacks and a small, but perfectly formed, menu.

9 La Caravella

MAP P5 ■ Via XXII Marzo, S Marco 2399 ■ 041 520 89 01 ■ €€€

Resembling a caravel sailing ship, this restaurant has trestle tables. The menu features Venetian dishes with a modern twist and a good wine list.

Alfresco dining at La Caravella

10 Acqua Pazza

MAP N5 ■ Campo Sant'Angelo, S Marco 3808/10 ■ 041 277 06 88 ■ Closed Mon, 7 Jan–7 Feb ■ €€€

Amalfi cuisine, including Neapolitan pizza, pasta and fish dishes, feature at this fine-dining restaurant.

See map on pp80–81

📕 San Polo and Santa Croce

Venice's greatest concentration of sights can be found in these neighbouring districts, at the geographical heart of Venice, having grown around the ancient core of Rialto where the first inhabitants settled. Here, glorious churches, landmark monuments and breathtaking palaces are all saturated in history. Essential sights include Santa Maria Gloriosa dei Frari, the Scuola Grande di San Rocco, where Tintoretto demonstrated his genius on sumptuous canvases, and the morning bustle of Rialto market. The squares of San Polo and San Giacomo dell'Orio are both full of cafés and benches for resting weary feet.

Campo San Giacomo dell'Orio

SAN POLO AND SANTA CROCE

1 The Rialto
See pp34–5.

2 Santa Maria Gloriosa dei Frari

Known by all simply as the Frari (a corruption of *Frati*, meaning "friars"), this huge, plain Gothic church (see pp32–3) dwarfs the eastern section of San Polo. The first church was built by Fransiscan friars during 1250–1338, but was replaced by a larger building, which was completed by the mid-15th century. The interior is striking for its sheer size and for the quality of its works of art. These include masterpieces by Titan and Giovanni Bellini, as well as Donatello's famous John the Baptist and a number of imposing monuments to famous Venetians. The campanile, set into the left transept of the church, is the second largest in the city.

Façade of Scuola Grande di San Rocco

3 Scuola Grande di San Rocco

MAP K4 ■ Campo S Rocco, S Polo 3052 ■ Open 9:30am–5:30pm daily ■ Closed 1 Jan, 25 Dec ■ Adm ■ www.scuolagrandesanrocco.org

Blinding in the morning sun, the early Renaissance façade of this historic building, home to master-pieces by Tintoretto, is a marvel of intertwined sculpted stone wreaths and crouching elephants dwarfed by stately columns. The Istrian stone facing is embedded with a medley of burgundy porphyry and green-and cream-veined marble inserts. Designed by Bartolomeo Bon in 1517 and added to by Scarpagnino among others, the imposing building with neighbour-ing church was home to one of the city's foremost confraternities, established in 1478, and honoured with an annual visit by the doge.

4 Campo San Giacomo dell'Orio

MAP L2

This quintessential picturesque square, well off the beaten track, sports plane trees, benches for relaxing and patches of grass. Modest surrounding palaces are home to Venice University's archi-tectural faculties. The laid-back air and abundance of restaurants and coffee shops make it very inviting, and there's no lack of subjects for photographers or artists.

5 Chiesa di San Giacomo dall'Orio

MAP L2 ▪ Campo S Giacomo dell'Orio, S Croce ▪ 041 275 04 62 ▪ Open 10:30am–1:30pm & 2:30–5pm Mon–Sat ▪ Adm ▪ www.chorusvenezia.org

Do not miss this unusual church. Founded in the 9th century, its Latin-cross shape features a marvellous 15th-century wood-beamed ceiling and a forest of colourful granite and black limestone columns from the Middle East, several of them loot from the Crusades. The floor merits close scrutiny for its multitude of fossils, while memorable paintings include Palma il Giovane's *Descent of Manna* (1580–81), left of the main altar, and a painted crucifix (1350) attributed to Paolo Veneziano.

6 Scuola Grande di San Giovanni Evangelista

MAP L3 ▪ Campiello della Scuola, S Polo 2454 ▪ 041 71 81 58 ▪ Open 9:30am–1pm & 2–5:15pm daily ▪ Adm ▪ www.scuolasangiovanni.it

This erstwhile confraternity headquarters with a high-ceilinged upstairs hall is mostly used for conferences. The monumental staircase was the work of Coducci and the priceless reliquary contains a fragment of the True Cross, presented to the Scuola in 1369. The spectacular *Miracles of the Cross* cycle of paintings commissioned of Gentile Bellini and associates is now in the Accademia Galleries *(see pp30–31)*. The exterior court-yard has a fine sculptured portal screen completed in 1485 by Pietro Lombardo mounted with an eagle to symbolize St John.

Scuola Grande di San Giovanni Evangelista

Grand setting of Palazzo Mocenigo

7 Palazzo Mocenigo

MAP M2 ▪ Salizzada S Stae, S Croce 1992 ▪ 041 72 17 98 ▪ Open 10am–5pm Tue–Sun (last admission 30 min before closing time) ▪ Closed 1 Jan, 1 May, 25 Dec ▪ Adm ▪ www.visitmuve.it

The richly furnished and frescoed rooms of this 18th-century patrician palace have showcases of historic fabrics and costumes, plus a fascinating history of perfumes. The Mocenigo family portrait gallery has a total of seven doges, topped in fame by Alvise I, the victor at the 1571 Battle of Lepanto against the Turks, which was crucial for the Republic.

8 Campo San Zan Degolà

MAP L1 ▪ Chiesa di San Giovanni Decollato: open 9am–4pm Mon–Sat

People usually hurry through this square en route to the bus terminal, oblivious to its quiet charm. Interest starts with the curious loggia on the western canal edge, then there's the attractive plain church named for San Giovanni Decollato or St John the Beheaded, depicted with flowing curly locks in a stone bas-relief on the southern wall. Inside the simple Veneto-Byzantine building are lovely 13th-century frescoes, an unusual survivor for damp old Venice.

9 Giardino Papadopoli
MAP J3

A leafy haven of twittering sparrows and flowerbeds close to Piazzale Roma and the car parks, these French-designed gardens date back to the 1800s when extravagant parties for the nobility were held here among various flower species and rare animals. Site of a demolished convent, it belonged to Corfuborn entrepreneurs, hence the Greek name. The public park was greatly reduced in size when the Rio Nuovo canal was excavated in 1932–3.

The lush Giardino Papadopoli

10 Ca' Pesaro Museo di Arte Orientale
MAP N1 ■ Fondamenta Ca'Pesaro, S Croce 2076 ■ Open 10am–5pm Tue–Sun (last admission 30 min before closing time) ■ Adm ■ www.visitmuve.it

This impressive Oriental Art Collection is an eclectic mix of 19th-century curiosities from all over the Far East. Exhibits include armour, porcelain and costumes, lacquerwork boxes and musical instruments. The museum is on the third floor, above the modern art gallery in Ca' Pesaro (see p24). A single ticket grants admission into the gallery and the museum.

A DAY IN SAN POLO

▶ **MORNING**

Before wandering east to Campo San Polo, stop at the **Scuola Grande di San Rocco** (see p89), to view Tintoretto's paintings, which are a sensory delight. Coffee is a must in the square, either at one of the local bars or at the attractive **Antica Birraria La Corte** (see p93).

It's not far from here to the **Rialto** market (see pp34–5) for late-morning bargains of fresh produce, often nearing half-price when stall-holders are in a hurry to shut up shop. If this has worked up an appetite, a Grand Canalside lunch is worth consideration at this point. There is a string of restaurants spread along the **Riva del Vin** (see p24), close to the foot of Rialto Bridge. Each displays live lobster and fish and has multilingual menus. In winter diners sit in see-through "tents" so that views of the canal and the procession of boats are ensured.

AFTERNOON

Head north and explore the craft and gift shops, lace, scarf and T-shirt stalls along Ruga Rialto and the old red-light area of **Rio Terrà Rampani** (see p60).

Try to end up in pretty **Campo San Giacomo dell'Orio** (see p89) for a pre-dinner drink at **Al Prosecco** wine bar (Campo S Giacomo dell'Orio, S Croce 1503; 041 524 02 22; closed Sun). Ask for a delicious glass of the fruity red Refosco from Friuli and bocconcino con mortadella di cinghiale (bite-sized roll with sliced wild boar).

See map on pp88–9

Craft Shops

1 Gilberto Penzo
MAP M3 ■ Calle Seconda
dei Saoneri, S Polo 2681■ Closed Sun
A visit to this workshop with
beautiful wooden models of traditional Venetian boats is a real treat.
Many crafts come in DIY kit form.

2 Mazzon le Borse
MAP L4 ■ Campiello S Tomà,
S Polo 2807 ■ Closed Sun
Papà Piero has been making
beautiful leather bags that last
a lifetime since 1963. His family
helps him in the workshop.

Hand-painting masks at Tragicomica

3 Tragicomica
MAP M4 ■ Calle dei Nomboli,
S Polo 2800 ■ Closed Sun
The result of 20 years of creating
elaborate papier-mâché and leather
masks and brocade costumes for
Carnival, as well as theatrical productions, can be appreciated in this
spectacular craft shop, where staff
explain the significance of pieces.

4 Marina e Susanna Sent
MAP P2 ■ Sottoportego del Rialto,
S Polo 70 ■ Closed Sat & Sun
Come here for strikingly simple but
exquisitely elegant necklaces and
earrings in clear and coloured glass.

5 Laberintho
MAP M2 ■ Calle del Scaleter,
S Polo 2236
Two goldsmiths create contemporary
jewellery pieces and replicas of
antique rings. For a special souvenir,
they will also make something
tailored to your specifications.

6 Sabbie e Nebbie
MAP M4 ■ Calle dei Nomboli,
S Polo 2768/A ■ Closed Sun
Customers come to this boutique
to purchase pottery, candles and
other trinkets from Japan and Italy.

7 Attombri
MAP P2 ■ Sottoportego degli
Orefici, S Polo 65 ■ Closed Sun
In an old covered passageway that
has long been home to the Rialto
Market goldsmiths, Attombri is
run by two designer brothers who
make limited-edition jewellery.

8 Cenerentola
MAP C4 ■ Calle dei Saoneri,
2718/A S. Polo ■ Closed Mon & Tue
A wide selection of Venetian fabrics,
lampshades and lamps to satisfy
every taste are sold at Cenerentola.

9 Margherita Rossetto Ceramica
MAP K2 ■ Corte Canal, S Croce 659
Eggcups, teapots and platters are
some of the delightful hand-turned
objects available here.

10 Gems of Venice
MAP N3 ■ Calle de l'ogio
1044, S Polo
At this boutique and workshop
precious gemstones are transformed
into works of art that can be worn.

Necklaces at
Gems of Venice

Places to Eat

PRICE CATEGORIES

For a three-course meal for one with half a bottle of wine (or equivalent meal), taxes and extra charges.

€ under €40   €€ €40–60   €€€ over €60

1 La Zucca
MAP L1 ■ Ponte del Megio, S Croce 1762 ■ 041 524 15 70 ■ Closed Sun ■ €€

Delicious vegetarian fare is served here, and there is also the promise of unforgettable chocolate desserts.

2 Osteria Bancogiro
MAP P2 ■ Campo S Giacometto, S Polo 122 ■ 041 523 20 61 ■ Closed Mon ■ €€

This is a trendy restaurant-bar along the Grand Canal serving a variety of quality Italian vintages and tasty nibbles.

Osteria Bancogiro

3 Da Fiore
MAP M3 ■ Calle dello Scaleter, S Polo 2202/A ■ 041 721 308 ■ Closed Sun & lunch (except Sat); 3 weeks in Jan; & Aug ■ €€€

The exclusive Da Fiore is possibly one of Venice's best restaurants. For great views, reserve the outdoor table on the balcony. Book in advance.

4 Il Refolo
MAP L2 ■ Campo San Giacomo dell'Orio, S Croce 1459 ■ 041 524 00 16 ■ €

Diners come to this great canal-side spot for inexpensive pizzas in a magical surrounding.

5 Osteria Mocenigo
MAP M1 ■ Salizzada San Stae, S Croce 1919 ■ 041 523 17 03 ■ €

Don't miss the *cestino al parmiggiano*, a crisp fried pastry and cheese basket filled with prawns at this traditional Venetian restaurant.

Elegant dining area at Muro

6 Muro
MAP N2 ■ Campiello dello Spezier, S Croce 2048 ■ 041 524 16 28 ■ €

Order steak or fish here – Antipasto Muro is a great seafood selection.

7 Antica Birraria La Corte
MAP M3 ■ Campo S Polo, S Polo 2168 ■ 041 275 05 70 ■ Closed Tue ■ €

Pizzas named after the city's bridges are served at this restaurant set in a former brewery. There is also a tree-shaded patio.

8 Gelateria Polo Nord
MAP B3 ■ Ramo Quinto Gallion O del Pezzetto, S Croce 273 ■ 348 033 25 08 ■ Closed Jan & Dec ■ €

This artisan *gelateria* serves *Crema Veneziana*, swirled with chocolate and candied orange, and *Budino Goloso*, which has Marsala wine and biscuits.

9 Taverna Da Baffo
MAP L3 ■ Campiello Sant'Agostin, S Polo 2346 ■ 041 524 20 61 ■ €

Seek out this tranquil square for a light lunch with a glass of Belgian beer or crisp Friuli wine.

10 Pasticceria Rizzardini
MAP M3 ■ Campiello dei Meloni, S Polo 1415 ■ Closed Tue, Aug ■ €

This old-style pastry shop serves thick hot chocolate and divine fruit tarts, almond slices and peanut toffee.

See map on pp88–9

TOP 10 Dorsoduro

Chiesa dei Gesuati, Zattere

A district of contrasts, Dorsoduro stretches from the port, via the panoramic Zattere and Grand Canal, all the way to the Punta della Dogana. Highlights for visitors include two foremost art galleries, the Accademia and the Peggy Guggenheim Collection, crammed with masterpieces ancient and modern, as well as Ca' Rezzonico palace and magnificent churches, Santa Maria della Salute and San Sebastiano, the latter famous for its wonderful Veronese works. Literally the "hard backbone" of Venice, built on elevated islands of compacted subsoil, Dorsoduro used to be sparsely populated. Today, as home to most of the city's university premises, it is full of lively cafés, bars and nightlife, concentrated in the market square, Campo Santa Margherita.

DORSODURO

Canale di Santa Maria Maggiore
RIO TERRA DEI PENSIERI
Rio della Cazziola
FMTA DI S M MAGGIORE
FMTA PAGNA
FMTA CAZZIOLA
FONDAMENTA DEL RIO NUOVO
C E CORTE BASEGO
Rio Nuovo
CPL MOSCA
CALLE DEI PRETI
Rio a
C SAN PANTALON
6 8
1
Rio di Ca' Foscari
FONDAMENTA DELLE PROCURATIE
C LARGA RAGUSEI
CALLE NUOVA
FMTA MALCANTON
C SAONERI
CALLE FOSCARI
FONDAMENTA DEI CERERI
Rio del Tintor
FONDAMENTA DELL'ARZERE
Rio dell'Arzere
FONDAMENTA ROSSA
CALLE RAGUSEI
7
CAMPO SANTA MARGHERITA
CAI BERNI
CALLE DEI GUARDIANI
Rio di S Margherita
CAMPO DEI CARMINI
RIO TERRASANT'APONAL
9
7
NUOVA TERESE
FMTA DEI BARI
Rio d. Terese
Rio del Carmini
FMTA DEL SOCCORSO
Rio Briati
CAMPO DEI CARMINI
FMTA DELLO SQUERO
FMTA GHERARDINI
3 4
CAMPO S BARNABA
8
CALLE D CERCHI
3
FONDAMENTA BARBARIGO
FONDAMENTA DE PESCHERIA
CORTE LARDONA
C. BEVILACQUA
CAMPO ANGELO RAFFAELE
FMTA SAN SEBASTIANO
Rio di San Nicolo
CALLE DELL'AVOGARIA
CALLE LUNGA SAN BARNABA
Rio
CAMPO SQUERO
2
FONDAMENTA EREMITE
FONDAMENTA DI BORGO
9
DORSODURO
5
C. BALASTRO
Rio Malpaga
2
SALIZZADA SAN BASEGIO
BANCHINA DEL PORTO COMMERCIALE
BANCHINA DI SAN BASEGIO
CALLE D MORTI
FMTA ZATTERE PONTE LUNGO
FONDAMENTA OGNISSANTI
Rio Ognissanti
CAMPO SA TROVASO
4
San Basilio
2
Zattere
Canale della Giudecca

---

1 **Top 10 Sights**
see pp97–9

1 **Places to Eat**
see p101

1 **Shops**
see p100

***Previous pages** Basilica di Santa Maria della Salute, from the Campanile di San Marco*

1 **Accademia Galleries**
See pp30–31.

2 **Zattere**
MAP C5

This broad waterfront took its name from the rafts of timber (*zattere*) floated downstream from the extensive forests in the northern Dolomite region which were managed by the Venetian Republic. The precious wood was either used for constructing palaces or transformed into masts and the like for the important shipbuilding industry. The tall-masted sailing ships and rowing boats that used to moor here have long since been replaced by motorized *vaporetti* and tourist launches, and nowadays the Zattere signifies lovely lagoon views and is perfect for a daytime or evening stroll.

3 **San Nicolò dei Mendicoli**
MAP A5 ■ Campo S Nicolò, Dorsoduro 1907 ■ 041 275 03 82 ■ Open 10am–noon & 3–5:30pm Mon–Sat; 9am–noon Sun & hols

This Veneto-Byzantine church with an imposing square *campanile* (bell tower) is known to film buffs from Nicholas Roeg's chilling 1973 horror film *Don't Look Now (see p65)*. Hidden in a maze of alleyways off the port zone, it has a pretty portico that doubled as a shelter for the poor. Founded in the 7th century, it is the second-oldest church in Venice. In the 1970s it was restored by the Venice in Peril Fund, who water-proofed the low floor.

San Nicolò dei Mendicoli

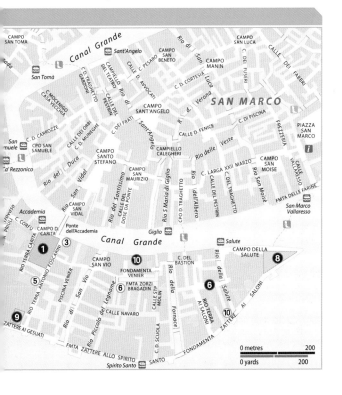

MASKS

Handmade in papier-mâché and glittery plaster, Venetian masks (**right**) are now strictly tourist fare, but they were once essential attire during Carnival, allowing aristocrats to enjoy themselves in anonymity. One unusual model, with a long curved nose, was used by doctors during plagues, its cavity filled with perfumed herbs to filter the diseased air.

4 Squero di San Trovaso
MAP C5

This is the city's most famous gondola repair and construction yard, though its days may be numbered. The combined workshop-dwelling is reminiscent of an Alpine chalet, as the first occupants came from the mountainous Cadore region. Closed to visitors, it backs on to a canal (Rio di San Trovaso), so it's easy to watch the caulking and cleaning in progress.

5 Chiesa di San Sebastiano
MAP B5 ■ Campo S Sebastiano, Dorsoduro 1907 ■ 041 275 04 62 ■ Open 10:30am–1:30pm & 2:30–5pm Mon–Sat ■ Adm ■ www.chorusvenezia.org

This 16th-century church (see p49) is a treasure trove of Paolo Veronese paintings. The artist devoted most of his life to its fresco cycle.

6 Rio Terrà dei Catecumeni
MAP D5

A reclaimed thoroughfare between the Zattere and Santa Maria della Salute, this stretch is dominated by a long building, now a school, where prisoners-of-war of the Republic who did not profess the Christian faith were held captive until they converted. This quiet backwater comes alive on 21 November with the Salute festivities (see p77).

7 Campo Santa Margherita

The sprawling square of Santa Margherita (see pp38–9), lined with houses from the 14th and 15th centuries, is the lively hub of western Dorsoduro. Market stalls, offbeat shops and cafés attract many young people. The colourful fish stalls sell live eels and lobster, the *erborista* alternative medicine, and the bakers some of the tastiest loaves in Venice. The former church of Santa Margherita, now an auditorium owned by the university, lies to the north of the square. Visitors can see sculptural fragments from the original 18th-century church, including gargoyles on the truncated campanile and adjacent house.

8 Punta della Dogana
MAP E5 ■ Campo della Salute, Dorsoduro 2 ■ 041 523 16 80 ■ Open 10am–7pm Wed–Mon ■ Adm ■ www.palazzograssi.it

This exciting addition to the Venetian contemporary art scene is housed in an imposing 17th-century customs building, the interior of which was restored by Japanese architect Tadao Ando. It contains important works, including pieces by British artists Rachel Whiteread and the Chapman Brothers, and offers fantastic views towards St Mark's, San Giorgio and the two main canals of Venice. Tickets also grant entry into the Palazzo Grassi (see p82).

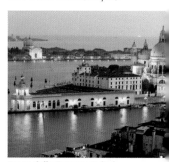

Punta della Dogana at dusk

Altar in Chiesa dei Gesuati

9 Chiesa dei Gesuati

MAP C5 ▪ Fondamente delle Zattere, Dorsoduro 917 ▪ 041 275 06 42 ▪ Open 10:30am–1:30pm & 2:30–5pm Mon–Sat ▪ Adm ▪ www.chorusvenezia.org

Set right on the Zattere waterfront close to the main ferry moorings, the Gesuati (also known as Santa Maria del Rosario) is often confused with the Gesuiti (Jesuit) establishment in Cannaregio. Taking over from a minor religious order, the Domenican friars had this church constructed in Classical style in 1726 by Giorgio Massari. Inside, the ceiling consists of three uplifting frescoes (1737–9) by Tiepolo, considered among his best work, portraying St Dominic amid glorious angels in flight.

10 Peggy Guggenheim Collection

Intended as a four-storey palace, this building never rose beyond the ground floor. It was in 1949, that the building was bought as a home by Peggy Guggenheim, a collector, dealer and patron of the arts. She had her vast collection of modern European and American art in this museum (see pp40–41), which was inaugurated in 1980. Today, Guggenheim remains Venice's most visited sights. The light-filled rooms and the modern canvases provide a striking contrast to the Renaissance paintings which are the main attraction in Venetian churches and museums.

EXPLORING DORSODURO

▶ MORNING

The **Accademia Galleries** (see pp30–31) can be overwhelming, so focus your visit on a selection of its masterpieces, but don't neglect the Carpaccios and Bellinis. After all that art, have a relaxing coffee watching the boats go by at **Snack Bar Accademia Foscarini** (Rio Terrà Antonio Foscarini, Dorsoduro 878/C; 041 522 72 81),a magical spot right at the foot of Accademia Bridge.

Next, head off east for a leisurely stroll, past Longhena's work of art, the church of **Santa Maria della Salute** (see p48), to **Punta della Dogana**, a great spot for taking photos of Piazza San Marco. Turn back in the direction of the **Zattere** (see p97) and Giudecca Canal. **Al Chioschetto** (Zattere, Dorsoduro 1406/A; closed Dec–mid-Jan), a bar right on the water's edge, is a good spot for lunch.

AFTERNOON

Wander through to **Campo Santa Margherita** to the **Scuola Grande dei Carmini** (see p38) to admire Tiepolo's canvases, then take some time to admire the architectural curiosities of this fascinating square.

As sunset approaches waste no time in occupying a table for a Spritz aperitivo at the trendy bar **Margaret DuChamp** (Campo S Margherita, Dorsoduro 3019; 041 528 62 55). It's hard to better this as a place for people-watching, and an added bonus is the scent of jasmine that fills the air as night falls.

See map on pp96–7

Shops

(1) 3856
MAP K4 ▪ Calle San Pantalon, Dorsoduro 3749 ▪ Closed Sun

A small but perfectly assembled selection of clothing and accessories is available at this shop run by a friendly mother-and-daughter team.

(2) Liberia Marco Polo
MAP B4 ▪ Campo Santa Margherita, Dorsoduro 2899

An independent bookshop, Liberia Marco Polo has new and second-hand books in Italian, English, French and German. Local poetry readings and book presentations are hosted here.

(3) Totem-Il Canale Gallery
MAP C5 ▪ Rio Terrà Antonio Foscarini, Dorsoduro 878/B ▪ Closed Tue

Bulky ancient beads, made with vitreous paste and once traded in Africa, count as precious antiques. There are modern African wood artworks too.

(4) Signor Blum
MAP K5 ▪ Campo S Barnaba, Dorsoduro 2840

Detailed jigsaw models of Gothic palaces, flanked by wall panels and painted toy figures are handmade by this co-operative of female artisans.

Signor Blum

(5) Augusto Mazzon
MAP L5 ▪ Calle del Traghetto, Dorsoduro 2783

Everyone's Christmas tree needs one of the joyous gilded cherubs lovingly crafted by wood-carver and painter Danilo. He also makes picture frames and furniture.

(6) Officina Veneziana
MAP K4 ▪ Campo S Pantalon, Dorsoduro 3701 ▪ Closed Sun

Choose from a wonderful selection of Art Deco jewellery, Easter eggs, Christmas decorations and fine china.

(7) Perla Madre Design
MAP K5 ▪ Calle delle Botteghe, Dorsoduro 3182▪ Closed Sun

Colourful glass bead jewellery is made right in front of your eyes by designer Simona Iacovazzi.

Trendy design shop Madera

(8) Madera
MAP K5 ▪ Campo S Barnaba, Dorsoduro 2762 ▪ Closed Sun

This contemporary design store has minimalist pieces in wood and glass, as well as gorgeous ceramics.

(9) Libreria Toletta
MAP L6 ▪ Sacca della Toletta, Dorsoduro 1213

Specializing in art and architecture, this popular bookshop also has a great collection of guidebooks and novels in English.

(10) Arras
MAP L5 ▪ Campiello Squelini, Dorsoduro 3235 ▪ Closed Sun

This shop stocks original hand-woven fabrics, garments and bags in beautiful colours.

Places to Eat

PRICE CATEGORIES

For a three-course meal for one with half a bottle of wine (or equivalent meal), taxes and extra charges.

€ under €40 ▪ €€ €40–60 ▪ €€€ over €60

1 Gelateria Nico
MAP C5
▪ Fondamenta Zattere, Dorsoduro 922 ▪ 041 522 52 93 ▪ €

This spot is Venice's most renowned ice-cream parlour (see p66). *Gianduiotto da passeggio* – hazelnut and chocolate ice cream smothered in whipped cream – is a local favourite.

Gianduiotto da passeggio

2 Osteria Enoteca Ai Artisti
MAP C5 ▪ Fondamenta della Toletta, Dorsoduro 1169/A ▪ 041 52 38 944 ▪ Closed Mon & Sun ▪ €€

Try the seafood ravioli in this cosy and welcoming canal-side restaurant.

3 La Bitta
MAP K6 ▪ Calle Lunga de San Barnaba, Dorsoduro 2753 ▪ 041 523 05 31 ▪ No credit cards ▪ Closed Sun ▪ €€

Fine Italian wines accompany a superb menu at this restaurant (see p69). Leave room for one of their delicious desserts.

4 Impronta Caffè
MAP K4 ▪ Calle dei Preti, Dorsoduro 3815 ▪ 041 275 03 86 ▪ Closed Sun ▪ €

Affordable meals and long opening hours make this a local favourite.

5 La Rivista
MAP C5 ▪ Rio Terrà Foscarini, Dorsoduro 979/A ▪ 041 240 14 25 ▪ Closed Mon & Sun pm ▪ €€

Innovative Italian cuisine is offered here, in relaxing, designer modern surroundings. There is an inspiring choice of cold platters of cheese and meats. The wine list is impressive.

6 Ai Gondolieri
MAP D5 ▪ Ponte del Formager, Dorsoduro 366 ▪ 041 528 63 96 ▪ €€

One of the city's top restaurants, Ai Gondolieri specializes in game from the Veneto when in season.

7 Bar alla Toletta
MAP L6 ▪ Dorsoduro 1191 ▪ €

Renowned for its wide range of sandwiches, which are fresh and generously filled.

8 Pasticceria Tonolo
MAP K4 ▪ Crosera S Pantalon, Dorsoduro 3764 ▪ 041 523 72 09 ▪ Closed Mon ▪ €

Try delicious, freshly baked almond biscuits and mini pizzas at one of the city's best pastry shops.

9 Gelateria Il Doge
MAP K5 ▪ Campo S Margherita, Dorsoduro 3058A ▪ 041 523 46 07 ▪ Closed Dec & Jan ▪ €

Treat yourself to the *Crema del Doge* (candied fruit, egg custard and chocolate) at this great ice-cream parlour (see p66).

10 Linea d'Ombra
MAP D5 ▪ Ponte dell'Umiltà, Dorsoduro 19 ▪ 041 241 18 81 ▪ Closed Wed ▪ €€€

Enjoy the waterside setting behind the landmark Salute church. Specialities on the menu include tuna tartare and sea bass in a salt crust.

Waterside seating, Linea d'Ombra

See map on pp96–7

⏻🔟 Cannaregio

Accounting for the huge crescent between the northern bank of the Grand Canal and the lagoon, the bustling *sestiere* of Cannaregio reaches from the railway station to the city hospital. It was home to Marco Polo and artists Titian and Tintoretto, and is home to landmark churches such as Madonna dell'Orto along with the old Jewish Ghetto. Named after the *canne* (reeds) that once filled its marshes, it is crossed by Strada Nova, the city's main thoroughfare, but also contains Venice's narrowest alley, the 58-cm- (23-inch-) wide Calle Varisco. This vibrant area has its own market, craft workshops and rowing clubs, while relaxation comes at the string of shady parks and laid-back cafés and bars that line the maze of backstreet canals.

Campo dei Mori

CANNAREGIO

1 Ca' d'Oro

MAP N1 ■ Calle Ca' d'Oro, Cannaregio 3932 ■ 041 520 03 45 ■ Open 10am–7pm Tue–Sun (last admission 6:30pm) ■ Closed 1 Jan, 1 May & 25 Dec ■ Adm ■ www.cadoro.org

Behind the resplendent palace's *(see p46)* Gothic tracery is a column-filled courtyard paved with coloured tesserae. Inside is the Galleria Giorgio Franchetti, a collection of paintings, sculptures and ceramics donated to the State by Baron Giorgio Franchetti in 1916, along with the building. One highlight is Andrea Mantegna's painting *St Sebastian* (1560) pierced by arrows "like a hedgehog", in the portico leading to a loggia overlooking the Grand Canal. An ornate 15th-century staircase leads to 16th-century Flemish tapestries on the second floor.

Jewish Ghetto, once a closed island

2 Jewish Ghetto

MAP C1 ■ Museo Ebraico, Campo del Ghetto Nuovo, Cannaregio 2902/B ■ 041 715 359 ■ Open 10am–5:30pm Sun–Fri (last admission 4pm) ■ Closed public and Jewish hols ■ Adm ■ www.museoebraico.it

The word "ghetto" originated in Venice, derived from *getto* (casting) due to an old iron foundry here. As of 1492, many Jewish refugees reached Venice after expulsion from Spain and in 1516 they were obliged by law to move to this area. Their movements around the city were restricted; they were subject to a curfew and forced to sleep behind locked gates. Waves of arrivals saw each language group build its own synagogue and raise the buildings to seven floors in height. Today, the city still has a thriving Jewish community, but few still live in the ghetto. The synagogues can be visited with a guide; don't miss, too, the Museo Ebraico (museum of sacred objects).

3 Corte Seconda del Milion

MAP Q2

The restructured Malibran Theatre, situated in this photogenic square, was erected in the 1790s on the site of a house, where the famous 13th-century explorer Marco Polo *(see p50)* was born. Other early Gothic buildings remain, their timber overhangs set off by bright-red geraniums. Along with the adjoining bridge, the square was named in honour of the explorer whose stories about the Orient in *Il Milione* continue to inspire travellers.

1 Top 10 Sights
see pp103–5

1 Places to Eat
see p107

1 Specialist Shops
see p106

Santa Maria dei Miracoli

4 Santa Maria dei Miracoli

MAP Q2 ■ Campo dei Miracoli, Cannaregio ■ 041 275 04 62 ■ Open 10:30am–1:30pm & 2:30–5pm Mon–Sat ■ Adm ■ www.chorusvenezia.org

A "jewellery box" of marble slabs and exquisite bas-reliefs, this Renaissance church (see p48) was named after a miracle-working icon from 1409, said to have resuscitated a drowned man and now enshrined in the main altar.

5 Campo dei Mori

MAP D1

In this odd, funnel-shaped square your attention is drawn to three statues of Arabian-style "Moors" – but neither North African nor Muslim, they hailed from Morea in Greece. Rioba, Sandi and Afani Mastelli were medieval traders who made their home in the family palace around the corner. Next to the bridge over Rio della Sensa is a doorway marked No. 3399, once the home of renowned 16th-century artist Tintoretto (see p54).

THE JEWS IN VENICE

Banned by Republic law from practising manual trades, many Jews were skilled doctors or moneylenders. Most were refugees from other parts of Europe, and they are credited with introducing rice-based dishes to Venetian cuisine. As remembered by a memorial in the former ghetto, few returned from the Nazi camps of World War II.

6 Farmacia Ponci

MAP D2 ■ Strada Nova, Cannaregio 2233/A

The "Casa degli Speziali", the oldest pharmacy in Venice, carries on its business along-side its restored 16th-century rooms. Displayed on original briarwood shelving adorned with Baroque statues in Arolla pine-wood are rows of 17th-century porcelain jars used for storing medicinal ingredients; for safety reasons, poisons were kept in a rear room. Pharmacies were strictly regulated and numbered 518 in 1564, the year their guild was formed.

7 Fondamente della Misericordia and degli Ormesini

MAP C2

Parallel to the Strada Nova but worlds away from the tourist bustle, these adjoining quaysides have a real neighbourhood feel. There's a good sprinkling of osterie (wine bars) along-side coffee houses and bookshops. The area enjoys a renaissance of sorts and foodies will be spoilt for choice. The word "ormesini" derives from a rich fabric traded through Hormuz, now in Iran, and imitated in Florence and Venice. Ormesini leads into Misericordia and to the towering red-brick Scuola Grande building. Used as the city's basket-ball team headquarters for many years, it occasionally opens for temporary exhibitions.

8 Palazzo Labia

MAP C2 ■ Campo S Geremia, Cannaregio ■ Closed to the public

Abandoned when its wealthy merchant owners fled to Vienna at the fall of the Republic, this 17th-century palace overlooking the Canal di Cannaregio acted as a silk factory, saw-mill and primary school, but was badly dam-aged in 1945 when a boat loaded with munitions blew up in front of it. Luckily, the wonderful ballroom frescoed by Tiepolo has been restored. The palace belongs to RAI, the state broadcasting service.

⑨ Chiesa di Sant'Alvise

MAP C1 ■ Campo S Alvise, Cannaregio ■ Open 10:30am–1:30pm & 2:30–5pm Mon–Sat ■ Adm ■ www.chorusvenezia.org

This church is said to have been commissioned by a Venetian noblewoman in 1388 to honour Saint Louis of Toulouse after the saint appeared to her in a dream. Major restoration took place in the 17th century, when the ceiling was painted with frescoes by Pietro Antonio Torri and Pietro Ricchi. Other notable works of art in the church include paintings by Giambattista Tiepolo – *Ascent to Calvary*, *Crowning with Thorns* and *The Flagellation*.

Ceiling fresco of Chiesa di Sant'Alvise

⑩ Fondamente Nuove

MAP E2

Opposite the cemetery island of San Michele *(see p118)*, this lagoon-side pavement is an important jumping-off point for ferries to the northern islands and sports one of the city's rare petrol stations. The ample quay-sides were not constructed and paved until the mid-1500s; until then the waterfront reached back to Titian's garden (No. 5113, Calle Larga dei Botteri), giving unobstructed views of the Alps on a clear day.

EXPLORING CANNAREGIO

▶ MORNING

Begin the day with the Galleria Franchetti in the lovely **Ca d'Oro** *(see p103)*, but leave plenty of time to explore the rest of the palace, making sure that you take in the balconies overlooking the Grand Canal and the mosaics in the courtyard. Afterwards, head to **Torrefazione Cannaregio** *(see p87)* for a cup of the best coffee in town. Only minutes away is the fascinating **Jewish Ghetto** *(see p103)*, where you can take an informative guided tour of the many remaining synagogues in the area.

For a revitalizing break, and a change from pasta and pizza, try **Orient Experience** *(Rio Terà Farsetti, Fondamenta di Cannaregio, Cannaregio 1847; 041 822 4337)* for lunch.

AFTERNOON

Wander up the canal towards the unusual, three-arched **Ponte dei Tre Archi** *(see p58)*. Return over the bridge and head for **Fondamenta della Sacca**, which affords good views of the Dolomites on a clear day. Many ways lead east from here, but try to take in the church of **Madonna dell'Orto** *(see p49)* for the Tintoretto paintings, then **Campo dei Mori** to see the house where the artist once lived.

On Fondamenta Ormesini, pop into **Al Timon** *(Fondamenta Ormesini, Cannaregio 2754; 041 524 60 66)*, where energetic waiters will serve you a glass of north Italian wine.

See map on pp102–3

Specialist Shops

1 Tà Kalà
MAP D2 ■ Strada Nova,
Cannaregio 4393/C
Close to Campo SS Apostoli, this
gift shop is a stockist of fascinating
holograms, Murano glass delights,
masks and chunky jewellery.

2 Mori & Bozzi
MAP D2 ■ Rio Terrà della
Maddalena, Cannaregio 2367
One of the best shoe shops in
Venice offers an irresistible
selection of women's footwear,
clothes and accessories.

3 San Leonardo Market
MAP C2 ■ Rio Terrà San
Leonardo ■ Mon–Sat
In the morning and late afternoon
this area functions as a lively open-
air produce market. In autumn
the air is thick with the aroma
of roasting chestnuts.

San Leonardo Market

4 Luna Darin
MAP C2 ■ Salizzada S Geremia,
Cannaregio 316
Come here for handmade glass beads
in brilliant hues and shapes, window
hangings and Christmas decorations.

5 Costumi Nicolao Atelier
MAP C1 ■ Fondamenta dei
Ormesini, Cannaregio 2590 ■ Closed
Sat & Sun
This is the place to go to hire a Carnival
outfit. It offers a wide range of period
costumes and formal evening wear. It
also organizes mask-making courses.

Paintings for sale at Codex

6 Codex
MAP C2 ■ Fondamenta
Ormesini, Cannaregio 2778
This studio and exhibition space of
resident artists Nelson Kishi and
Robin Frood sells original drawings,
paintings, prints and posters.

7 Miani
MAP Q2 ■ Salizzada S Canciano,
Canareggio 5577 ■ Closed Sun
Handmade Murano glass beads are
turned into beautiful jewellery by the
family that runs this shop. Try to
catch a demonstration.

8 Salmoiraghi & Viganò
MAP D2 ■ Strada Nova,
Cannaregio 3928–3930
Italian spectacles are stylish
and good value, and this well-
reputed optometrist can make up
prescription glasses the same day.

9 Arte Ebraica Shalom
MAP C1 ■ Ghetto Vecchio,
Cannaregio 1218 ■ Closed Sat &
Jewish hols
An artisan shop that specializes in
Jewish handicrafts such as menorahs
made with Murano glass or bronze,
and mezuzahs with mosaic designs.

10 Gianni Basso
MAP E2 ■ Calle del Fumo,
Cannaregio 5306 ■ Closed Sat
pm & Sun
The handmade stationery on offer at
this shop is made by a modest artisan
and is popular with international VIPs.

Places to Eat

1 **Il Paradiso Perduto**
MAP D2 ▪ Fondamenta della Misericordia 2540, Cannaregio ▪ 041 720 581 ▪ Closed Tue & Wed ▪ €

An osteria with a menu that changes daily. Try the *il gran fritoin*, a fried fish made with white polenta.

2 **Grom**
MAP B3 ▪ Fondamente S Lucia, Cannaregio 1 ▪ €

Ice creams, sorbets, milkshakes and more are served at this branch of the popular Italian gelato chain.

3 **Ostaria Boccadoro**
MAP E3 ▪ Campo Widman, Cannaregio 5405 ▪ 041 521 10 21 ▪ €€€

Pasta dishes and delicate blends of seafood and seasonal vegetables are on offer here *(see p68)*, as well as desserts and an extensive wine list.

4 **Taverna del Campiello Remer**
MAP D3 ▪ Campiello Remer, Cannaregio 5701 ▪ 041 522 87 89 ▪ €€€

This converted warehouse has upturned barrels as tables and offers a delicious buffet menu.

5 **Il Santo Bevitore**
MAP D2 ▪ Campo S Fosca, Cannaregio 2393 ▪ €

Enjoy a drink and snack at this laid-back bar with live music. There is a good range of quality beers.

6 **Vini da Gigio**
MAP D2 ▪ Fondamenta S Felice, Cannaregio 3628/A ▪ 041 528 51 40 ▪ Closed Mon & Tue, 2 weeks in Aug ▪ €€

Canal-side restaurant *(see pp68–9)* serving innovative traditional dishes.

7 **Al Parlamento**
MAP B2 ▪ Fondamenta Savorgnan, Cannaregio 511 ▪ 041 244 02 14 ▪ €

Appetizing, simple meals are served at this café set beside the canal.

PRICE CATEGORIES
For a three-course meal for one with half a bottle of wine (or equivalent meal), taxes and extra charges.

€ under €40 €€ €40–60 €€€ over €60

Canal-side dining tables at Da Rioba

8 **Da Rioba**
MAP D2 ▪ Fondamenta Misericordia, Cannaregio 2553 ▪ 041 524 43 79 ▪ Closed Mon ▪ €€–€€€

The impeccably presented Venetian fish-based dishes on the menu at this restaurant are given a tasteful modern twist.

9 **Osteria Anice Stellato**
MAP C1 ▪ Fondamenta della Sensa, Cannaregio 3272 ▪ 041 720 744 ▪ Closed Mon & Sun, 2 weeks in Aug ▪ €€

It is important to book well ahead for this popular place. Among the culinary delights on offer are fish and meat dishes, as well as a wonderful *zabaglione* dessert.

10 **La Bottega Ai Promessi Sposi**
MAP P1 ▪ Calle dell'Oca, Cannaregio 4367 ▪ 041 241 27 47 ▪ Closed Mon lunch ▪ €

This low-key restaurant offers diners tasty *cicchetti* (bar snacks) while friendly staff serve more substantial traditional Venetian fare.

See map on pp102–3

TOP 10 Castello

Named after a castle possibly built here in Roman times, Castello is the "fishtail" of Venice. The western half of the district is crammed with historic highlights such as the churches of SS Giovanni e Paolo and San Zaccaria. However, half of Castello is taken up with shipbuilding, focusing on the historic Arsenale. The tree-lined Giardini is the venue for the Biennale art exhibition.

Riva degli Schiavoni

CASTELLO

1 Riva degli Schiavoni
MAP F4

Thronging with tour groups and packed with souvenir stalls, this quayside affords a lovely promenade past majestic palaces (now mostly hotels) and a much photographed 1887 monument to the first king of Italy, Vittorio Emanuele. It is linked to Piazza San Marco by the elegant Istrian stone bridge Ponte della Paglia, named after the *paglia* (straw) once unloaded from barges here. This is also the best place for taking pictures of the Bridge of Sighs. At the eastern end is the Ca' di Dio ("house of God"), a 13th-century hospice for pilgrims en route to the Holy Land.

2 Hotel Danieli
This enchanting 15th-century palace with a pink Gothic façade is set on the magnificent waterfront near Piazza San Marco. After a string of aristocratic proprietors, it was taken over in 1822 by Joseph da Niel, who turned it into a hotel *(see p146)* with an illustrious guest list, including Dickens, Wagner and Ruskin. In the 1940s an annexe was added amid great controversy – since 1102 no dwelling over one floor had been allowed on the site. The redeeming feature of the 1940s wing is the roof restaurant.

Eye-catching front of Hotel Danieli

3 Santa Maria della Pietà
MAP F4 ■ Riva degli Schiavoni, Castello 3701 ■ Open 10:15am–noon & 3–5pm Tue–Fri (to 1pm & 2–5pm Sat & Sun) ■ Adm ■ www.pietavenezia.org

Inextricably linked with the composer and musician Antonio Vivaldi, this Classical-fronted church designed by Giorgio Massari belonged to the adjoining home for foundlings where he taught. It is best seen by attending an evening concert to appreciate Tiepolo's ceiling fresco, exalting music and the young choristers, identifiable by the sprigs of pomegranate blossom they wear. The choir stalls accommodated both the singers and the nobility, who were not expected to mix with the commoners.

Nuove

RSENALE

Dársena Grande

Rio de San Gerolamo

S. STRETTA

Canale di San Pietro

Rio di San Pietro

CAMPO SAN PIETRO

5

NDAMENTA RSENALE

Tana

CAMPO DI RUGA

Rio di Sant'Anna

G. GARIBALDI

9

VIALE GIUSEPPE GARIBALDI

CALLE ANCORE

CALLE CORRERA

SECO MARINA

TE MARTIRI

4

2

Santa Maria della Pietà

4 Arsenale
MAP G3 ■ Castello

Aptly named after the Arab word *darsina'a* ("house of industry"), Venice's formidable Arsenale ship-yards at their peak employed an army of 16,000 to produce the fleets that sailed the Mediterranean, spreading and protecting the influence of the Republic through trade deals and naval superiority. With its innovative assembly-line system, the Arsenale could construct a galley in a few hours, notably in 1574 while the French king Henry III enjoyed a banquet. The stone lions that guard the entrance hail from Greek islands looted by Venetian commanders.

Crenellated entrance to Arsenale

5 San Pietro di Castello
MAP H4 ■ Chiesa di San Pietro di Castello ■ Open 10:30am–1:30pm & 2:30–5pm Mon–Sat ■ Adm ■ www.chorusvenezia.org

It is hard to imagine that Venice's religious headquarters were here until 1807, when the Basilica di San Marco became the city's cathedral. Linked to the rest of Castello by two broad bridges, San Pietro attracts artists for its evocative, forlorn air, and fun-lovers for the late-June neighbourhood fair. Art lovers come for the church with work by Veronese and Coducci.

6 Campo Santi Giovanni e Paolo
MAP E3

Dominated by the brick façade of the Gothic church SS Giovanni e Paolo, this

Campo Santi Giovanni e Paolo

square welcomes visitors with a flotilla of outdoor cafés. Worthy of contemplation is one of the world's most magnificent equestrian statues, a stylized 15th-century portrait of the great *condottiere* (mercenary leader) Bartolomeo Colleoni. He left a legacy to the city on the condition that his statue be erected in front of San Marco, craftily "interpreted" by the governors as the nearby Scuola Grande di San Marco. Decorated with arches and trompe l'oeil panels by Lombard masters, this former confraternity serves as the public hospital.

7 Campo Santa Maria Formosa
MAP E3 ■ Chiesa di Santa Maria Formosa ■ Open 10:30am–1:30pm & 2:30–5pm Mon–Sat ■ Adm ■ www.chorusvenezia.org

A lovely rounded church on this sun-blessed square appears to spread in all directions, the result of a 7th-century bishop's vision of the *formosa* ("shapely") Virgin Mary's request that it be built where "a white cloud came to rest". Artworks are by Vivarini and Palma il Vecchio. The square is a good place for a picnic or a game of football, in lieu of the bullfights and re-enactments of Venice's conquests held here in the olden days.

8 Chiesa di San Francesco della Vigna
MAP F3 ■ Campo S Francesco della Vigna, Castello 2786 ■ 041 520 61 02 ■ Open 10am–4pm Mon-Sun

In the back alleys of Castello, this Franciscan church sports a combination of architectural styles courtesy of both Sansovino and Palladio *(see p55)*, who designed the façade. The colonnaded cloister can be seen while you're admiring Giovanni Bellini's *Madonna and Child* (1507). Another highlight is Veronese's *Virgin and Child with Saints* (1551). Playgrounds have replaced the 13th-century *vigna* (vineyard).

9 Via Garibaldi and Giardini

MAP H5

A pleasant avenue lined with cafés and a market, Via Garibaldi was named when the eponymous general marched into Venice in 1866 as part of his campaign for Unification. Take a stroll to the Giardini (public gardens). To make way for the park in 1807, architect Selva (see p55) demolished four churches and convents and a sailors' hospice.

Via Garibaldi

10 Ospedaletto

MAP F3 ▪ Barbaria delle Tole, Castello 6691 ▪ Open for pre-booked guided tours only (email: booking@fondazioneveneziaservizi.it) ▪ Adm

The sculptures on the façade of this almshouse church, built in 1575, were added by Longhena in 1674. Pass through the church to the Sala della Musica, where female wards of the orphanage once gave concerts.

THE VENICE BIENNALE

The Giardini and its beautiful tree-lined avenues (below) were inaugurated as an international exhibition area in 1895 under the entrepreneur Count Volpi di Misurata. Every two years, more than 50 countries send artists to represent them, each with their own pavilion custom-designed by some of the world's leading architects, such as Alvar Aalto, Carlo Scarpa and James Stirling.

A DAY IN CASTELLO

▶ MORNING

After a visit to the Gothic church on **Campo Santi Giovanni e Paolo**, wander through the city's hospital. Although it is now ultra-modern inside, you can still appreciate the wonderful Renaissance façade, and a series of ancient courtyards and confraternity buildings. Continue the historic theme with a coffee and cake at old-style **Rosa Salva** (Campo SS Giovanni e Paolo, Castello 6779; 041 522 79 49).

Take a stroll, via **Campo Santa Maria Formosa**, to Campo San Zaccaria and the church with its Bellini painting, and **Scuola di San Giorgio degli Schiavoni** (see p57) for its Carpaccio works. For lunch, **Via Garibaldi** is a good bet, at one of the cafés or at **Il Nuovo Galeon** (041 520 46 56).

AFTERNOON

Head east along **Via Garibaldi**, and detour briefly into the shady avenue for the statue of Giuseppe Garibaldi and his followers. After a visit to the island of **San Pietro di Castello**, make your way back via the lagoon and the **Giardini**. A poignant sculpture to the female partisans of World War II can be seen at water level.

Head in the direction of San Marco, just past the mouth of Via Garibaldi. On the embankment is **Angiò Bar** (Riva di S Biasio, Castello 2142; 041 277 85 55; closed Tue), the perfect spot for a Venetian sunset together with a glass of wine, not to mention all manner of delicious snacks.

See map on pp108–9

Specialist Shops

1 Le Ceramiche
MAP F4 ■ Calle del Pestrin, Castello 3876 ■ Closed Wed & Thu

Alessandro Merlin crafts original plates, cups and tiles with black and white designs based on lagoon fish or human figures in this tiny atelier close to the Arsenale (see p110).

2 VizioVirtù Cioccolateria
MAP E3 ■ Calle Forneri, Castello 5988

This artisan chocolate factory creates chocolates from traditional Venetian recipes. Specialities include spiced hot chocolate and pralines. Book a tasting tour at info@viziovirtu.com.

3 Papier Mâché
MAP R3 ■ Calle Lunga Santa Maria Formosa, Castello 5174

One of the few traditional mask shops in town also sells beautiful ceramics.

4 Manufactus Venezia
MAP E4 ■ Calle delle Bande, Castello 5275

A traditional bookbindery where you can also find leather bags and accessories designed and made in Italy.

5 Il Ponte dei Sogni
MAP F4 ■ Salita Sant'Antonin, Castello 3473 ■ Closed Sun

Filled with Venice-themed gifts for both children and adults, most of the items here are handmade by the shop owner.

6 Libreria Acqua Alta
MAP R3 ■ Calle Lunga Santa Maria Formosa, Castello 5176

With ancient volumes piled high and Venetian-specific literature,

Staircase of books, Libreria Acqua Alta

Libreria Acqua Alta is a fascinating bookshop that has a gondola full of books inside.

7 Muranero
MAP F4 ■ Salizzada del Pignater, Castello 3545 ■ Closed Sun–Tue

Senegalese artist Niang Moulaye creates beautiful handmade jewellery, combining African style with Murano glass bead-making techniques.

Venetian mask

8 Ratti
MAP F4 ■ Salizzada S Lio, Castello 5825 ■ Closed Sun

This eclectic shop sells household items such as the quintessential Italian coffee pot, along with mobile phones and hardware.

9 Corte delle Fate
MAP E3 ■ Salizzada S Lio, Castello 5690

Ultra-modern footwear and quirky accessories are available here in the shape of bags, jewellery and on-trend clothing.

10 Giovanna Zanella
MAP Q3 ■ Calle Carminati, Castello 5641 ■ Closed Sun

A must for all serious shoppers, this store offers quirky handmade shoes in a fabulous range of incredible designs.

Places to Eat

PRICE CATEGORIES

For a three-course meal for one with half a bottle of wine (or equivalent meal), taxes and extra charges.

€ under €40 €€ €40–60 €€€ over €60

1 Corte Sconta
MAP F4 ■ Calle del Pestrin, Castello 3886 ■ 041 522 70 24 ■ Closed Sun & Mon, Jan, mid-Jul–mid-Aug ■ €€€

One of Venice's finest restaurants, Corte Sconta is known for its delicious seafood antipasti. Book in advance.

2 Caffè La Serra
MAP H5 ■ Viale Giuseppe Garibaldi, Castello 1254 ■ 041 296 03 60 ■ €

Housed in a former greenhouse, La Serra is perfect for a light snack after exploring the gardens of the Biennale.

3 Gelateria Gallonetto
MAP E3 ■ Salizada S Lio, Castello 6727 ■ 041 847 69 76 ■ Closed Dec & Jan ■ €

Enjoy creamy, delcious ice cream made with fresh products here. The fruit-rich sorbets, the Grand Crus dark chocolate and the fresh mascarpone cream are all excellent.

4 Trattoria dai Tosi Piccoli
MAP H5 ■ Secco Marina, Castello 736–738 ■ 041 523 71 02 ■ Closed Wed & 25 Dec ■ €

This cheery restaurant is especially popular during the Biennale art exhibition (see p76). Mouthwatering *pasta della casa* (house pasta) includes seafood and vegetables. There is a pizza menu at dinner.

5 Osteria Santa Marina
MAP Q2 ■ Campo S Marina, Castello 5911 ■ 041 528 52 39 ■ Closed Sun; Mon lunch, 2 weeks in Jan ■ €€€

Sample creative versions of Venetian and Italian fare at this well-reputed restaurant. In summer, diners can enjoy candlelight dining outside.

6 Alla Rivetta
MAP E4 ■ Ponte S Provolo, Castello 4625 ■ 041 528 73 02 ■ Closed Mon ■ €€

This friendly joint has good seafood options and regional dishes.

7 Alla Mascareta
MAP E3 ■ Calle Lunga S Maria Formosa, Castello 5183 ■ 041 523 07 44 ■ Closed lunch ■ €

An upmarket bar for wine lovers, Alla Mascareta also serves antipasti and main dishes.

Cosy interior of Alla Mascareta

8 Alle Testiere
MAP E3 ■ Calle del Mondo Nuovo, Castello 5801 ■ 041 522 72 20 ■ Closed Mon, Aug, 23 Dec–10 Jan ■ €€€

There is an unusual selection of fish, cheese and wines here.

9 Nevodi Pizza Lab
MAP G4 ■ Via Giuseppe Garibaldi, Castello 1342 ■ 045 238 173 ■ Closed Mon ■ €

This takeaway pizzeria has an excellent *mozzarella in carrozza* (fried cheese sandwich) and aubergine parmigiana.

10 Al Covo
MAP F4 ■ Campiello de la Pescaria, Castello 3968 ■ 041 522 38 12 ■ Closed Tue & Wed, 1 week Aug, 4 weeks Dec–Jan ■ €€€

Come here for sophisticated fish dishes and pair them with choices from the Italian wine list.

See map on pp108–9

TOP 10 The Northern Lagoon

The northern lagoon is dotted with mud flats and abandoned islands where rambling monasteries lie crumbling in the sun, backed by sweeping views of snow-capped mountains. Refugees from the mainland, fleeing the Huns, first settled on Torcello, which grew with the additional influx of influential religious orders. Today, however, only a handful of islands are still inhabited – glassmaking Murano is the most important, while Burano, Mazzorbo and Sant'Erasmo have skeletal populations of fishers and market gardeners. Salt pans, such as Le Saline, were a source of employment until as late as 1913.

Glass birds on Murano

THE NORTHERN LAGOON

Murano

Canale degli Angeli
Venier ③
CPO SAN DONATO
Da Mula ② ② ④
⑥ Museo
①
Serenella 🚢 ④ Murano ③
Navagero 🚢
FONDAMENTA VETRAI
CALLE BRESSAGIO
③
🚢 Faro
⑤
⑦ ①
🚢 Colonna

0 metres 400
0 yards 400

Torcello ①
Torcello 🚢 ⑨

Mazzorbo 🚢 Burano
Mazzorbo ④ ② Burano
⑥ ⑦ ⑩ ⑤ ⑧ ⑧ ⑨ ⑩

San Francesco del Deserto ⑤

🚢 Punta Vela

Laguna Veneto

See Murano inset, above
Murano

Lazzaretto Nuovo
🚢 Chiesa
Lazzaretto Nuovo 🚢 ⑧
🚢 Capannone
⑦ Sant'Erasmo

Punta Sabbioni ⑩
Punta Sabbioni 🚢

Cimitero 🚢
🚢 San Michele ⑥
Fondamente Nove 🚢

Le Vignole
Vignole 🚢

VENICE

S. Pietro
Certosa 🚢 ⑨ Certosa

0 kilometres 1
0 miles 1

Lido

①	**Top 10 Sights** see pp117–19
①	**Places to Eat** see p121
①	**Specialist Shops** see p120

Previous pages Cappella degli Scrovegni, Padua

1 Torcello
See pp36–7.

2 Burano
MAP H1 ■ Ferry No. 12 from Fondamente Nuove or S Zaccaria

A haven for artists, Burano takes pride in its brightly painted houses, fish and lace-making. The islanders cherish an old legend about a faithful sailor who resisted the Sirens' call and was rewarded with a magnificent veil of magical foam for his bride, later worked into lace, a trade that brought worldwide fame and fortune to the isolated fisherfolk. These days, old women still strain their eyes with patient stitches, but many articles are imported from abroad. The island's dramatically leaning bell tower is visible from afar.

3 Murano
MAP G2 ■ Vaporetto lines 4.1 & 4.2 from Fondamente Nuove & S Zaccaria, 3 from P Roma or seasonal lines

Long synonymous with glassmaking, Murano brought blowing as well as fusion techniques to extraordinary heights in the 1500s, and so closely guarded were the trade secrets that skilled crafters could migrate only under pain of death. Though Venice's glass monopoly lasted only until the 17th century, its fame lives on. A visit to the Museo del Vetro (Glass Museum) with its 4,000 exhibits *(see p56)* is a must. Don't be put off by the reps who invite tourists to see a furnace and showroom; it's a unique opportunity to watch the glassblowers at work and is free. However, if you accept a free boat trip from San Marco to a glass factory, you're expected to make your own way back by *vaporetto* if you don't buy anything. Glassmaking aside, Murano is a lovely place with canals, alleyways and friendly islanders.

4 Mazzorbo
MAP H1 ■ Ferry No. 12 from Fondamente Nuove

This pretty, verdant island exudes a tranquil air as locals tend their vineyards or artichoke fields.

Wicker cages for fattening up *moleche* (soft-shelled crabs) hang over the water and the produce can be sampled in the low-key trattorias. Amid the scattering of houses are bold modern council blocks, which are painted in pastel hues. Mazzorbo has its own boat stop but is also joined to Burano by a long timber footbridge.

Waterfront of Mazzorbo

5 San Francesco del Deserto
MAP H1 ■ Taxi launch from Burano's landing stage ■ Monastery: open 9–11am, 3–5pm Tue–Sun ■ Donation ■ www.sanfrancescodeldeserto.it

A short distance from Burano, this attractive island of cypress trees is home to a Franciscan monastery. According to legend it was founded by St Francis in person, on his way back from preaching missions in Egypt and Palestine in 1220. In May, clad in their brown habits and sandals, the monks attend the Vogalonga regatta *(see p76)* in their heavy-duty boat, much to the delight of the Venetian crowds.

San Francesco del Deserto

Verdant San Michele cemetery

6 San Michele

MAP G2 ■ Ferry Nos. 4.1 & 4.2 from Fondamente Nove & S Zaccaria ■ Cemetery: open 7:30am– 6pm daily (Oct–Mar: to 4:30pm)

San Michele became the city cemetery in 1826, in the wake of a Napoleonic decree that the dead should be buried far from city dwellings to improve hygiene standards. Entry to the cemetery is via a beautiful Gothic portal surmounted by St Michael at odds with a dragon, and through the monk's colonnaded cloister. But don't neglect to visit the pretty marble-façaded church next door, designed by Mauro Coducci (see p55) in 1469. On All Souls' Day (2 November), the place is crowded

with relatives paying a visit to their dear departed. However, unless you're a famous resident like Ezra Pound, Igor Stravinsky or Sergei Diaghilev, your bones are dug up after 10 years and placed in an urn to make room for someone else.

7 Sant'Erasmo

MAP H2 ■ Ferry No. 13 from Fondamente Nuove

Just over 4 km (2.5 miles) long and 1 km (0.5 miles) at the broadest point, Sant'Erasmo offers tranquil countryside, praised enthusiastically by the Romans who built sumptuous villas here. A couple of rickety old motorcars occasionally bump along the lanes, but bicycles and boats are still the main form of transport. The main activity here is market gardening, particularly the production of delicious asparagus and artichokes, which prosper on the sandy soil and are a mainstay of Rialto Market (see p34). There is also a small stretch of sandy beach.

Asparagus and artichokes

8 Lazzaretto Nuovo

MAP H2 ■ Ferry No. 13 from Fondamente Nuove ■ Tours: Apr–Oct (by reservation only, call 041 244 40 11) ■ www.lazzarettoveneziani.it

Up until the 1700s this island, across the water from Sant'Erasmo, served as a quarantine station for merchant ships entering the lagoon and suspected of carrying the plague. Together with Sant'Erasmo it held up to 10,000 people during the 1576 pestilence, while cargoes were fumigated with rosemary and juniper in temporary shelters. Later converted into a military stronghold,

---

LAGOON FLORA AND FAUNA

The lagoon abounds in gilt-head bream, sea bass, clams, cuttlefish and crabs, all prey for wetland waterfowl such as swans, egrets (**below**), cormorants and the rare black-winged stilts. Sea lavender blooms on land masses, rock samphire clings to crumbling masonry, while glasswort thrives in the salt-ridden marshes.

it now swarms with archaeology enthusiasts, intent on unearthing its secrets, and Italian students attending summer camps.

Certosa
MAP H2 ▪ Alilaguna: www. alilaguna.it

Inhabited by religious communities for more than 600 years, the "charterhouse" island went the way of many of its neighbours under occupation by French, Austrian and Italian forces, though currently as the property of the City Council it is slowly being cleaned up as a public park. It can be visited in summer months, though opening times vary; Alilaguna's Linea Blu boats stop here seasonally. From the Lido–Punta Sabbioni ferry the impressive ramparts of Sanmicheli's 16th-century Forte di Sant'Andrea can be seen, much as they must have appeared in the past to any hostile vessels that dared to enter the lagoon unbidden.

Punta Sabbioni
Ferry No. 14 from Lido & S Zaccaria

This locality clings to the promontory extending westward from the mainland – a continuous string of beach resorts equipped with spacious campsites. Alongside sleepy backwaters and canals is Punta Sabbioni ("big sandy point"), a busy bus-ferry terminal that bustles with summer holiday-makers. It came into being as sand accumulated behind the 1,100-m (3,600-ft) breakwater erected to protect the port mouth and littoral. The stretch offers some lovely seaside strolls.

Serene setting of Punta Sabbioni

SAILING THE LAGOON

▶ **MORNING**

To save money, buy a one-day travel card and then take a *vaporetto* from Fondamente Nove to **Murano** *(see p117)* to watch a glassmaking demonstration at a furnace or one of the workshops. Don't miss Murano's very own **Grand Canal** *(see pp24–5)*, before returning via Fondamenta Manin with its medieval porticoes for the turn-off towards the **Faro** (lighthouse) landing stage. **Bar al Faro** *(Fondamenta Piave 20, Murano; 041 739 724)* is a perfect spot for coffee.

Take a ferry to **Burano** *(see p117)*. Either picnic on the famous Burano biscuits or have lunch at **Da Romano** *(Piazza Galuppi 221, Burano; 041 730 030; closed Tue & Sun dinner, mid-Dec–early Feb dinner)*, which is a popular meeting place for artists.

AFTERNOON

Pop over to **Torcello** *(see pp36–7)* by ferry for the awe-inspiring Byzantine mosaics in the basilica. Climb the bell tower for views of the lagoon and the Dolomite mountains, if weather conditions and visibility are favourable.

Take the ferry back to **Burano** *(see p117)* and then head east, past low-lying islands and tidal flats towards Treporti. A stretch parallel to the sandy littoral separating the lagoon from the Adriatic Sea takes you to **Punta Sabbioni**, where a stopover is feasible for a drink on the jetty.

End the day sailing across the broad lagoon mouth, via the **Lido** *(see p123)*, back to **Piazza San Marco** *(see pp20–23)*.

See map on p116 ←

Specialist Shops

1 Cesare Sent
MAP G2
■ Fondamenta Vetrai 8B, Murano

This talented artist from a long line of glassmakers transforms the ancient art of mur-rhine glassware into striking modern objects of beauty.

Cesare Sent glasswork

2 ArtStudio
MAP G2
■ Fondamenta Rivalonga 48, Murano

Watch glass artist Davide Penso at work producing marvellous African-inspired glass beads.

3 Manin 56
MAP G2 ■ Fondamenta Manin 56, Murano

Striking etched bowls and slender wine glasses from Salviati flank international designer items in this wonderful collection.

4 Nason & Moretti
MAP G2 ■ Calle Dietro Gli Orti 12, Murano ■ Closed Sat & Sun

This small shop stocks a stunning collection of glassware created by these acclaimed Murano designers in a dazzling array of colours and styles. It is well worth visiting.

5 Barovier & Toso
MAP G2 ■ Fondamenta Vetrai 28, Murano

The oldest family of glassmakers in the world, the Baroviers are able to trace their ancestry back to the 13th century. They still produce stunning contemporary pieces.

6 Mazzega
MAP G2 ■ Fondamenta da Mula 147, Murano

Vast showrooms at Mazzega display traditional and semi-modern glass designs, with an emphasis on chandeliers and vases.

7 CAM
MAP G2 ■ Piazzale Colonna 1, Murano

This is the first shop visitors see as they disembark at the Murano Colonna stop. It is an internationally known firm specializing in distinctive high-quality, modern pieces.

8 Pastificio e Panificio Giorgio Garbo
MAP H1 ■ Via S Mauro 336, Burano

Sample some *bussolai*, Burano's trademark vanilla-flavoured short-bread, freshly baked in traditional rounds or "S" shapes.

9 Emilia Burano
MAP H1 ■ Via Galuppi 205, Burano

Superb laceware and exquisite in-house designed linen collections are sold at this family-run boutique.

10 Lidia Merletti d'Arte
MAP H1 ■ Via Galuppi 215, Burano

While the front of this shop is an emporium of lace tablecloths, hand towels and mats, the rear has a gallery with a priceless 18th-century wedding gown, a lace fan owned by Louis XIV and lace altarpieces.

Lidia Merletti d'Arte

Places to Eat

1 Trattoria Busa alla Torre, Da Lele

MAP G2 ■ Campo S Stefano 3, Murano ■ 041 739 662 ■ Closed dinner ■ €

Dine inside under timber rafters or out in the square. Start with ravioli filled with fish, but leave room for the nougat pastries.

2 Panificio Giovanni Marcato

MAP G2 ■ Fondamenta Rivalonga 16, Murano ■ 041 739 176 ■ Closed dinner ■ €

Pizza with tomato and olives, *zaletti* biscuits and *pincetto* (sponge cake with chocolate) feature on the menu among other delicious offerings.

3 Osteria La Perla Ai Bisatei

MAP G2 ■ Campo S Bernardo 6, Murano ■ 041 739 528 ■ Closed dinner & Wed ■ No credit cards ■ €

The *fritto misto* seafood is superb at this restaurant offering home-style cooking at reasonable prices.

4 Trattoria Valmarana

MAP G2 ■ Fondamenta Navagero 31, Murano ■ 041 739 313 ■ Closed Sun–Thu dinner ■ €

Rombo al forno con patate e olive (flounder with olives and potatoes) is a speciality at this stylish restaurant with a waterside terrace.

5 Trattoria Da Romano

MAP H1 ■ Via San Martino Destra 221, Burano ■ 041 730 030 ■ Closed Tue, Sun eve; mid Oct–mid Apr: dinner ■ €€€

This family-run trattoria is known for its *risotto di gò*, made with a tiny lagoon fish. It is frequented by celebrities such as Robert De Niro.

6 Riva Rosa Ristorante

MAP H1 ■ Via S Mauro 296, Burano ■ 041 730 850 ■ Closed Wed, Mon–Fri dinner ■ €€€

Try the Rossini *aperitivo* with freshly juiced strawberries and prosecco at this romantic canalside restaurant.

Antica Trattoria alla Maddalena

7 Antica Trattoria alla Maddalena

MAP H1 ■ Fondamenta S Caterina 7B, Mazzorbo ■ 041 730 151 ■ Closed Thu, Wed dinner ■ €

Try the spring artichokes or the roast duck with a light, local white wine at this restaurant. Book in advance.

8 Al Gatto Nero

MAP H1 ■ Fondamenta Giudecca 88, Burano ■ 041 730 120 ■ Closed Mon; dinner Wed, Thu & Sun; 1st week in Jul & Nov ■ €€

This alfresco fish restaurant serves fresh seafood and homemade pasta.

9 Locanda Cipriani

MAP H1 ■ Piazza S Fosca 29, Torcello ■ 041 730 150 ■ Closed Jan–Feb; Tue & dinner Sun–Thu & Mar, Nov & Dec ■ €€€

The house speciality here is *filetto di San Pietro Carlina* (baked John Dory with tomato and capers).

10 Venissa

MAP H1 ■ Fondamenta S Caterina 3, Mazzorbo ■ 041 527 22 81 ■ Restaurant: closed Dec–Feb, Tue & Wed; Osteria: closed Tue & Wed ■ €€€

Choose between the low-key *osteria* and the sophisticated restaurant serving locally grown produce.

See map on pp116

🔟 The Southern Lagoon and Venice Lido

The southern lagoon enjoys protection from the Adriatic Sea with shifting sand spits long transformed into a permanent littoral, the residential Lido, with the help of nature and man. The latter's efforts date back to the 6th century, but the earth and wicker barriers have since been modified to sturdy seawalls and massive parallel breakwaters at the shipping entrances of San Nicolò, Alberoni and Chioggia. On the lagoon's southwestern edge are fish farms and wild shallows where hunters and fishers still roam, well clear of the Valle Averto reserve run by the World Wildlife Fund for Nature (WWF).

Chiesa del Santissimo Redentore, Giudecca

Closer to Venice itself is a cluster of sizeable islands such as majestic San Giorgio and populous Giudecca, then diminutive land masses such as Lazzaretto Vecchio, where plague victims were once quarantined but which has now been re-adapted as a home for stray dogs. Elsewhere, a sanatorium has become a resort and there are countless other evocative abandoned places.

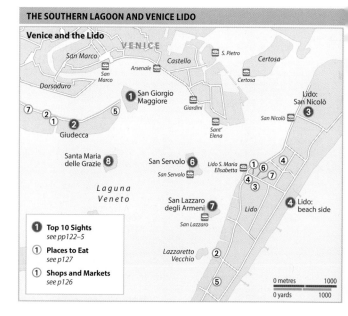

THE SOUTHERN LAGOON AND VENICE LIDO

Venice and the Lido

VENICE

San Marco

Dorsoduro

San Marco

Arsenale

Castello

S. Pietro

Certosa

Certosa

① San Giorgio Maggiore

Giardini

Lido: San Nicolò

San Nicolò ③

⑦ ② ①

⑤

② Giudecca

Sant' Elena

Santa Maria delle Grazie ⑧

San Servolo ⑥

San Servolo

Lido S. Maria Elisabetta ① ⑥

④ ④

④ ⑦

Laguna Veneto

San Lazzaro degli Armeni ⑦

San Lazzaro

Lido

④ Lido: beach side

Lazzaretto Vecchio ②

⑤

① **Top 10 Sights**
see pp122–5

① **Places to Eat**
see p127

① **Shops and Markets**
see p126

0 metres   1000
0 yards   1000

Interior of San Giorgio Maggiore

1 San Giorgio Maggiore
Fondazione Giorgio Cini
(vaporetto No. 2) ▪ 041 528 7827
▪ Open 10am–6pm daily ▪ Adm

The island of cypresses is separated from the main body of Venice by St Mark's Basin and retains a quiet, almost meditative air. An ancient vineyard and salt pans were replaced by a landmark church by Andrea Palladio (see p55) in the 16th century, adjoining an elegant Benedictine monastery. It is now a scientific and cultural foundation and conference centre. At the rear is the open-air Teatro Verde, which is used for performances of contemporary dance and music.

2 Giudecca
Vaporetto
Nos. 2, 4.1, 4.2

An S-shaped slice of land facing the sun-blessed Zattere, this residential garden island was first known as "Spina longa" for its fishbone form. It was renamed either after an early Jewish community or the *giudicati* (radical aristocrats) exiled here. The famous Italian Renaissance artist Michelangelo spent three peaceful years here in voluntary exile from 1529. Much later it became an important industrial zone with shipbuilding and the immense Molino Stucky flour mill. Usually quiet and neighbourly, it comes to life with a vengeance for the mid-July Redentore festivities (see p76).

3 Lido: San Nicolò
Jewish Cemetery: Bus A from S Maria Elisabetta or car ferry from Tronchetto ▪ Guided visits to the cemetery Mar–Oct (book ahead: 041 715 359) ▪ www.museoebraico.it

The northern end of the Lido littoral, a key point in the Republic's defence, used to be equipped with impressive naval fortifications, and chains would be laid across the lagoon mouth as a deterrent to invaders. The historic Festa della Sensa celebration (see p76) is held offshore from the church of San Nicolò, founded in 1044 and a former Benedictine monastery, now a study centre. One visitable site is the 1386 Jewish cemetery. Alternatively, take a 35-minute mini cruise on the car ferry between Tronchetto car park and San Nicolò. Its high decks offer great views.

The Southern Lagoon

Area shown on map, left
Venice
Lido
Fusina
Laguna Veneto
3
5 Malamocco
Alberoni
Golfo di Venezia
6 9 San Pietro in Volta
9 Pellestrina
8 9 10
8 9 10
10 Chioggia
0 km 3
0 miles 3

San Nicolò, Lido

HEYDAY OF THE LIDO

Evidence of the Lido's "golden age" as Europe's leading seaside resort at the turn of the 20th century can still be seen in the magnificent Art Deco villas. Exemplary survivors are the Hotel des Bains and the Excelsior, built in 1907 as the world's largest hotel, complete with mock minarets. Before that, the Lido was appreciated for its healthy air.

4 Lido: Beach Side
Ferry Nos. 1, 5.1, 5.2, 6, 14

Manicured sand, raked daily, and neat rows of multicoloured bathing cabins and beach umbrellas sum up the Lido from June to September, made famous in Thomas Mann's novel *Death in Venice (see p52)*. Venetians spend their summers socializing in style here. Things liven up considerably for the 10-day International Film Festival in September *(see p64)*, when the shady streets are filled with film buffs and critics on bicycles.

5 Lido: Malamocco
Bus No. 11 or line B from S Maria Elisabetta

About midway along the Lido is the pretty, quiet village of Malamocco and it's now hard to imagine that it was the most important lagoon settlement soon after Roman times and the main port for Padua. A storm and giant waves washed away the entire town in 1106, but it was later rebuilt in the vicinity on a smaller scale. It is appreciated for its 15th-century buildings, peaceful nature and rustic trattorias.

6 San Servolo
Ferry No. 20 from San Zaccaria ■ Open 11:30am & 2:45pm Mon–Sun; Sat & Sun guided visits only (book ahead: 041 862 71 67) ■ Adm

In 1648, 200 nuns exiled from Candia, Crete, by the Turks were lodged on this island, but after their numbers dwindled in 1725 it was given over to a sanatorium for psychiatric cases, although exclusively those of "comfortable circumstances". The roomy buildings are now shared by an international university and a trade school for artisans from all over Europe interested in restoration of stone and stucco techniques.

Student painting at San Servolo

7 San Lazzaro degli Armeni
Ferry line No. 20 from San Zaccaria ■ 041 526 01 04 ■ Open by appointment only ■ Adm ■ www.mechitar.org

Venice made a gift of this erstwhile leper colony to the Armenian monk, the Venerable Mechtar, forced out of the Peloponnese during one of his country's diasporas. Intent on fostering the Armenian culture and language, he founded a religious community here and set up a printing press that ran until 1994. Multilingual monks instruct visitors in Armenian history and lead tours through a small museum and a library of more than 100,000 volumes and precious illuminated manuscripts.

San Lazzaro degli Armeni

8 Santa Maria delle Grazie
Close to San Giorgio, this abandoned island used to be a hospice for pilgrims and was named after a miraculous image of the Virgin brought back from Constantinople and attributed to St Luke. Its colourful history features a series of religious orders and

churches, devastating fires, allotments, luxuriant gardens and the city's infectious diseases hospital. It is now private property with no public access.

⑨ San Pietro in Volta and Pellestrina

Bus-ferry No. 11 from the Lido or from Chioggia

This narrow 11-km (6.5-mile) central strip of land, linked to the Lido and Chioggia by ferry, is dotted with picturesque sleepy fishing communities, once famous for lacemaking and now renowned for champion rowers and a shipyard. The Genoese wiped out the villages during the 14th century, an event almost repeated during the disastrous 1966 floods – powerful waves broke over the seawall, forcing full-scale evacuation. The massive defensive barriers with their 14-m (46-ft) broad base were first erected in the 1700s, but have consequently needed large-scale reinforcement.

⑩ Chioggia

Ferry from Pellestrina or bus from Piazzale Roma

A lively fishing town, Chioggia has elegant bridges over navigable canals. The friendly inhabitants have a reputation for lawlessness and bickering, and speak a distinctive dialect with a singsong inflection. Chioggia's greatest moment came as the arena for the decisive battle in the 1378–9 war, when the Genoese came close to conquering Venice. In flat-bottomed boats the crafty locals lured the enemy into the lagoon, thus gaining the upper hand.

Cleaning fishing nets in Chioggia

A DAY ON THE LAGOON

Malamocco
Alberoni
BUS
FERRY
Laguna
Veneto
San Pietro in Volta
BUS
Golfo di
Venezia
FERRY
Pellestrina
Chioggia

▶ MORNING

From the Santa Maria Elisabetta ferry stop, either hire a bicycle or take bus B southwest along the lagoon edge for **Malamocco**. Wander through the peaceful village and over its bridge to the sea to take in the Adriatic and the impressive seawall. Then proceed with buses B or 11 through Alberoni and past the golf course for the vehicle ferry across the lagoon entrance. Get off at the second stop for **San Pietro in Volta**. Climb the high seawall for panoramic views of the sea, before turning lagoon-wards for the picturesque pastel-painted fishing settlement that spreads along the waterfront.

Have lunch at one of the great trattorias (see p127) or a sandwich and glass of wine at one of the modest waterfront bars.

AFTERNOON

Further south the bus terminates at **Pellestrina**, a brightly painted fishing village flanked by an active shipyard. The passenger ferry to **Chioggia** is a beautiful half-hour cruise past mussel grounds punctuated with fisher huts perched on poles, via the Ca' Roman landing stage, which provides access to a beach. Chioggia is a lovely town to explore, with its traffic-free piazza lined with old palazzos and countless fish restaurants.

Indulge in a pre-dinner drink and some *cicchetti* (bar snacks) at one of the laid-back cafés in the elegant Corso del Popolo.

See map on pp122–3

Shops and Markets

Double bicycles for hire in Lido

① Lido on Bike
MAP H2 ■ Gran Viale Santa Maria Elisabetta 21/B, Lido ■ Closed Nov–Feb

This well-stocked bike shop rents out all normal steeds as well as 4-wheeler family models.

② General Market
MAP H2 ■ Via Falier, Lido ■ Open Tue am

Open-sided vans sell fresh produce, alongside designer-quality clothes, shoes and bags at reasonable prices. Even if you don't buy anything, the lagoon setting makes a trip to this market worthwhile.

③ La Spiga Erboristeria
MAP H2 ■ Via Lepanto 5, Lido ■ Closed Mon, Sun

You will find Erbolario natural beauty products and plant-based cosmetics, as well as natural remedies for minor aliments here..

④ Arbor
MAP H2 ■ Gran Viale Santa Maria Elisabetta 10, Lido

The upmarket range of clothes at this shop attracts both foreign and Italian customers.

⑤ Salumeria Da Ciano
MAP H2 ■ Via Sandro Gallo, 156A, Lido

This delicatessen stocks gourmet Italian food products including mozzarella, ham, handmade pasta and artisan biscuits. Fresh ready-made Italian dishes can also be bought.

⑥ OVS & Conad
MAP H2 ■ Gran Viale Santa Maria Elisabetta 21/B, Lido

OVS, a store with fashionable, moderately priced clothing for all ages, is combined with Conad, a supermarket with a great selection of fresh produce.

⑦ Benetton
MAP H2 ■ Gran Viale Santa Maria Elisabetta 47/A, Lido

Despite being small, this shop is well-stocked with underwear, nightwear and swimwear.

⑧ El Penelo
MAP F2 ■ 577 Borgo San Giovanni, Chioggia ■ Closed Wed & Sun

Giorgio Boscolo is an expert in crafting traditional fishers' clay pipes – and he is the only craftsman who still makes them in terracotta and coloured glazes.

⑨ Venturini Souvenirs
MAP F1 ■ Corso del Popolo 1349, Chioggia

Ignore the trinkets here and instead focus on the intricately hand-crafted models of colourful *bragozzo* boats (see p26).

A boat model at Venturini Souvenirs

⑩ Panificio Da Sergio
MAP F1 ■ Stradale Ponte Caneva 626, Chioggia ■ Closed Mon

The dry biscuits sold here were traditionally made for seafarers. *Pevarini* are spicy rings with molasses and aniseed, while *Dolce del Doge* is spread with a chocolate-hazelnut mixture.

Places to Eat

PRICE CATEGORIES

For a three-course meal for one with half a bottle of wine (or equivalent meal), taxes and extra charges.
....
€ under €40 ■ €€ €40–60 ■ €€€ over €60

1 Trattoria Altanella
MAP E6 ■ Calle delle Erbe, Giudecca 268 ■ 041 522 77 80 ■ Closed Mon & Tue, 10–20 Aug, Dec & Feb ■ €€€

Treat yourself to a candlelit dinner on the terrace. Fish dishes such as *frittura mista* (assorted fried seafood) are the speciality.

2 Ai Cacciatori
MAP D6 ■ Fondamenta Ponte Piccolo Giudecca 320 ■ 041 528 58 49 ■ Closed Mon, 15 Dec–15 Jan ■ €€€

Enjoy hearty Venetian fare such as *gnocchi con nero di seppia* (potato dumplings with cuttlefish ink) in canal-side seating with lovely views.

3 Trattoria da Scarso
MAP H2 ■ Piazzale Malamocco 5, Malamocco ■ 041 770 834 ■ Closed Mon dinner, Tue, Jan, Dec ■ €

The good-value family-run Trattoria Scarso has a lovely garden hung with fishing nets where you can linger over grilled fish or a fresh salad.

4 Trattoria La Battigia
MAP H2 ■ Via Nicosia 10, Lido ■ 041 528 06 15 ■ Closed Mon ■ €€

Renowned for its traditional fish dishes and friendly atmosphere, this trattoria is the place to enjoy *schie con* polenta, gray shrimps typical of the Venetian lagoon.

5 Hotel Cipriani
MAP E6 ■ Giudecca 10 ■ 041 240 801 ■ Closed Nov–Mar ■ €€€

Savour an artistic tasting menu at Michelin-starred Oro Restaurant, sip a mocktail at Cip's Club, or have a rustic dinner at Giudecca 10, Hotel Cipriani *(see p68)* is the perfect venue for every mood.

6 Ristorante da Memo
Via Portosecco 157, S Pietro in Volta ■ 041 527 91 25 ■ Closed Tue, Nov–Mar ■ €€

Try the fresh shrimps, eel or sole at this modest seafood restaurant with outdoor tables.

Excellent view from Harry's Dolci

7 Harry's Dolci
MAP C6 ■ Fondamenta S. Biagio, Giudecca 773 ■ 041 522 48 44 ■ Closed Nov–Easter ■ €€€

With views across the Giudecca Canal, this is the "sweet" branch of Harry's Bar *(see p25)*, for sorbets and pastries.

8 Ristorante La Sgura
MAP F1 ■ Fondamenta Marangoni 1295, Chioggia ■ 041 403 232 ■ Closed Mon, Jan ■ €

Situated on a quiet canal, this place also has a great selection of meat. Try the *zuppa di pesce* (fish soup).

9 Ristorante El Gato
MAP F1 ■ Corso del Popolo 653, Chioggia ■ 041 400 265 ■ Closed Mon, 15–28 Feb ■ €€

With a long-standing reputation for excellence, this restaurant serves superb *frittura* (fried fish), fish risotto and sautéed mussels and clams.

10 Trattoria La Nassa
MAP F1 ■ Calle Ponte Caneva 625, Chioggia ■ 041 400 861 ■ €

A family-run restaurant, Trattoria La Nassa serves a good selection of raw and cooked seafood dishes.

See map on pp122–3

TOP 10 Padua, Vicenza and Verona

A wealth of art cities punctuates the fertile Veneto plain that stretches in a broad wedge north from the Po River to the foothills of the Dolomites. There is evidence of the presence of Romans and Venetians alike in the shape of fascinating amphitheatres and elegant palaces in cities such as Verona and Vicenza, both of which have been declared World Heritage Sites by UNESCO. Moreover, amid vineyards of grapes, pressed for light sparkling prosecco and aromatic Bardolino, are charming, little-visited villas with ornamental gardens. Each town has its distinctive character: Padua, a business hub but with a richly artistic and religious heart; Vicenza, famous for its goldsmiths and Andrea Palladio's architecture; and romantic Verona, lazing on the banks of the mighty Adige River as it flows south swollen with snow-melt from the Alps. The highlights in each city can easily be visited as day-trips from Venice by train.

Piazza dei Signori

PADUA, VICENZA AND VERONA

1 Top 10 Sights
see pp129–31

1 Places to Eat
see p135

1 Veneto Shops
see p134

1 Villas
see pp132–3

Fresco in the Cappella degli Scrovegni

1 Cappella degli Scrovegni
Piazza Eremitani, Padua
■ Bus Nos. 3, 10, 12 ■ 049 201 00 20
■ Open 9am–7pm daily (booking
essential) ■ Adm ■ www.cappella
degliscrovegni.it

The sky-blue vault studded with gold
stars in this glorious Paduan chapel
seems to hover over Giotto's vibrant
frescoes, which narrate the lives of
Mary and Jesus. The Florentine
artist (1266–1337)
was summoned by
Enrico Scrovegni to
work on the chapel in
1305–6, to atone for
the sins of his late
father, a moneylender.
Especially noteworthy
among the 38 distinct
scenes is the *Last
Judgment* on the
entrance wall, with
its ranks of helmeted,
haloed and shield-
bearing angels. Book well in advance
in summer. Visits last 30–35 minutes,
including a 15-minute wait in the
"decontamination" chamber.

2 Palazzo Bo
Via VIII Febbraio 2, Padua
■ Bus Nos. 3, 12 ■ 049 827 39 39
■ Guided tours: daily ■ Adm ■ www.
unipd.it/visitebo

The original lectern where Galileo
Galilei held his lessons between
1592 and 1610 can be seen on the
guided tour of Padua's historic
university, founded in 1222 and
second only to Bologna as Italy's
and the world's oldest. The insti-
tution has the world's first anatomy
theatre (1594) where dissections
had to be carried out in great
secrecy as the church forbade such
practices. Other illustrious scholars
of the university have included
astronomer Copernicus (1473–1543),
Gabriel Fallopius (1523–62), who discovered the function of the Fallopian
tubes, and Elena Lucrezia Corner
Piscopia *(see p50)* – the world's
first woman graduate.

Anatomy theatre, Padua's University

ROMEO AND JULIET

There is no doubt that the Capulet and Montague families existed, though they were probably more friendly than William Shakespeare made out in his 1594–5 tragedy. However, the world's most famous star-crossed lovers may have come from Vicenza, the home town of Luigi Da Porto, author of the original 1530 account.

3 Casa di Giulietta
Via Cappello 23, Verona ■ Open 9am–7pm Tue–Sun ■ Adm ■ www.casadigiulietta.comune.verona.it

Visitors flock to "Juliet's House", the 13th-century presumed abode of the Shakespearean heroine, complete with a pretty balcony (added in 1928) from which you may imagine her uttering that immortal cry: "Romeo, Romeo, wherefore art thou Romeo?" The courtyard walls are filled with multilingual graffiti left by lovers from all over the world.

Juliet statue

4 Basilica del Santo
Piazza del Santo, Padua ■ Bus Nos. 3, 18 ■ Open 9am–1pm & 2–6pm Tue–Sun ■ www.basilicadelsanto.org

Popularly referred to as "il Santo", Padua's revered site of pilgrimage was built in the 13th century to safeguard the mortal remains of St Anthony, a Franciscan monk and miracle worker from Portugal. Devotees visit his gleaming tomb, encircled by burning candles, but his tongue is guarded in an intricate reliquary in the Treasury, recovered after being stolen. Inside you will find artworks by Sansovino, Tiepolo and Titian (see p54).

5 Piazza dei Signori
Basilica Palladiana: Piazza dei Signori, Vicenza ■ Open during exhibitions ■ Adm

In addition to the cafés in Vicenza's main square, visitors can admire the buildings by Palladio, whose 16th-century designs went on to influence both his home town and architecture worldwide (see p55). The basilica has twin levels of colonnaded arches, opposite Palladio's Loggia del Capitaniato. A statue of the architect can be found in the piazzetta at the western end.

6 Palazzo Leoni Montanari
Contra' Santa Corona 25, Vicenza ■ Open 10am–6pm Tue–Sun ■ Adm ■ www.gallerieditalia.com

On the entrance portal of this lavishly decorated Baroque palace are carvings of writhing serpents, and Hercules is shown in the act of slaying the Hydra on the loggia. The gallery's masterpieces include 120 awe-inspiring Russian icons and 14 fascinating paintings by Pietro Longhi depicting scenes from 18th-century Venetian life.

7 Verona Arena
Piazza Brà, Verona ■ 045 800 51 51 ■ Open 9am–7pm Tue–Sun ■ Adm ■ www.arena.it

This massive Roman amphitheatre dating from the 1st century CE measures almost 140 m (460 ft) in length. The impressive arcades and 44-level tiered seating for 22,000 people, that once rang with the cries of gladiator fights, now echo with arias from operas during the popular summer festival. Verdi's *Aida* has opened the festival every year since 1913. Visitors should note that the opening hours are shorter during the opera festival in the summer.

Visitors outside Verona Arena

⑧ Teatro Olimpico

Piazza Matteotti 11, Vicenza
■ Open 9am–5pm Tue–Sun (Jul–Aug: 10am–6pm; last admission 30 min before closing time) ■ Adm ■ www. teatrolimpicovicenza.it

A castle courtyard draped with creepers was chosen for this Vicenza theatre, designed by Palladio. The performing area is based on a Roman model, while the stage scenery represents the city of Thebes, built for 1585's inaugural play, Sophocles' *Oedipus Rex*. Scaled statues and varying stage levels create clever tricks of perspective.

Piazza delle Erbe in Verona

⑨ Piazza delle Erbe

Torre dei Lamberti, Cortile Mercato Vecchio, Verona ■ Open 10am–6pm Mon–Fri, 11am–7pm Sat & Sun; last admission 45 min before closing time ■ Adm ■ www.torredeilamberti.it

Originally Verona's Roman forum, this square is still a great spot for discussing business over a coffee. Parasols shade souvenirs at the market, watched over by a winged lion atop a column, a vestige of Venetian domination. The 84-m (275-ft) Torre dei Lamberti offers great city views.

⑩ Museo di Storia Naturale

Lungadige Porta Vittoria 9, Verona ■ Open 10am–6pm Tue–Sun (last admission 5:30pm) ■ Adm

Gigantic ferns, weird fish and an ancestor of the crocodile, all in fossilized form from the Eocene era 50 million years ago, are treasures hailing from Bolca in the Lessini foothills on display here. They testify to the tropical shallows that spread across the area prior to the formation of the Alps.

A DAY OUT IN VERONA

▶ **MORNING**

Where better to begin than the inspiring **Verona Arena**, where, as entertainment, wild animals once made a meal of gladiators? Afterwards, relax in the sun with a creamy coffee at **Liston 12 Caffè** *(Piazza Brà 12, Verona; 045 803 11 68)* and dig into a freshly baked jam-filled croissant.

A short stroll leads past the boutiques in the traffic-free Via Mazzini, paved with pink-tinged local limestone embedded with ammonite fossils, to **Casa di Giulietta** to the right, or **Piazza delle Erbe** and its elegant palaces to the left.

Backtrack to Via Mazzini for lunch at **Ristorante Greppia** *(Vicolo Samaritana 3, Verona; 045 800 45 77; closed Mon)* for *bollito misto* (mixed boiled meat) served with a traditional peppery sauce.

AFTERNOON

To digest lunch, head over the Adige River via the ancient Ponte di Pietra to the **Teatro Romano** on Via Rigaste Redentore – well worth a visit even if you're not in town for a summer evening performance. Then follow the river or walk back through town and west towards the medieval **Ponte Scaligero**, part of the adjoining castle. The triple-arched construction was blown up by the German army in World War II, then rebuilt brick by brick by town members.

The bridge leads to **Castelvecchio** for a timely *aperitivo* with a glass of white Soave wine at any of the welcoming bars.

See map on pp128–9

Veneto Villas

1 Villa Barbaro

Via Cornuda 7, Maser, bus from Treviso railway station ■ Open Apr–Oct: 10am–6pm Tue–Sun; Nov–Mar: 11am–5pm Sat, Sun & public hols ■ Adm ■ www.villadimaser.it

The best preserved villa (1560) by Palladio (see p55) lies close to the pretty hill town of Asolo. This charming country house features all manner of Roman-inspired elements, from the nymphaeum and grotto to the circular temple akin to the Pantheon. Playful trompe l'oeil frescoes by Veronese (see p54) adorn the six main rooms, counting amongst the most important works of art of the Venetian Renaissance, while the garden is punctuated with Classical statuary. Drop in to the estate's wine cellar in a farm house next door for wine tastings.

Villa Barbaro

has 114 sumptuously furnished rooms and a ballroom decorated by Tiepolo. Above the huge façade columns, scores of statues line the roof overlooking inner courtyards and a spacious park where the Venetian nobility would promenade on summer evenings. Be sure to explore the wonderful 1721 circular maze. The guest list has included one-time proprietor Napoleon, Russian and Austrian royalty, Mussolini and Hitler among others.

3 Villa Valmarana "Ai Nani"

Via dei Nani 8, Vicenza ■ Open Mar–Oct: 10am–6pm daily; (Nov–Feb: to 4pm Mon–Fri, to 5pm Sat & Sun) ■ Adm ■ www.villavalmarana.com

Known for the jaunty statues of dwarfs on the garden wall, these cosy twin buildings, built by the Valmarana family, stand on a pretty ridge looking up to Monte Berico and its sanctuary. The Tiepolo father and son fresco team were invited here by Count Valmarana in 1757 to decorate the main part and the guest quarters.

4 Villa Valmarana "La Rotonda"

Via Rotonda 45, Vicenza (bus No. 8) ■ Villa: open 10am–noon & 3–6pm Wed, Sat & Sun (Dec–mid-Mar: 10am–noon & 2:30–5pm); garden: open Tue, Thu, Fri & Sun same hours as villa (times may vary, check website) ■ Adm ■ www.villalarotonda.it

The perfectly proportioned imposing Villa Valmarana with four temple façades sits on a hill overlooking the architect Palladio's adoptive town of Vicenza. The house has been imitated throughout the world. If you want to visit the villa itself as opposed to the rather limited grounds, beware it's only open two days a week.

Villa Pisani – La Nazionale

2 Villa Pisani – La Nazionale

Via Doge Pisani 7, Strà ■ Villa & park: open mid-Mar–Sep: 9am–8pm Tue–Sun (Oct: to 7pm); Nov–mid-Mar: 9am–2pm Tue–Thu (to 6pm Fri–Sun & park to 5pm; last admission an hour before closing time) ■ Adm ■ www. villapisani.beniculturali.it

This splendid two-floor 18th-century villa designed for Doge Alvise Pisani

5 Villa Foscari "La Malcontenta"

Via dei Turisti 9, Malcontenta ■ Open Apr–Oct: 9am–noon Mon–Tue, Thu, Sat & Sun; 2:30–5:30pm Wed–Sun ■ Adm ■ www.lamalcontenta.com

Located on the bend of the Brenta Canal, but now rather too close to the Marghera industrial area, this wonderful residence designed by Andrea Palladio in 1571 is one of his best-known creations. It has a Greek temple façade, while the interior is decorated with frescoes. The name is said to refer to the "discontent" of a female member of the Foscari family, exiled here for adultery.

6 Villa Barbarigo

Galzignano, Valsanzibio ■ Open Mar–Nov: 10am–sunset daily ■ Adm ■ www.valsanzibiogiardino.it

The Euganean Hills are the setting for this Baroque garden, designed for the Venetian Barbarigo family by Luigi Bernini, architect of the Vatican fountains in Rome. The villa, dating from 1669, is a private dwelling, but the 15-ha (37-acre) garden provides a boxwood maze, fountains, fish ponds, statues and hundreds of trees.

7 Villa Emo

Via Stazione 5, Fanzolo di Vedelago ■ Open Mar–Oct: 10am–6pm Mon–Sun (last admission 5:30pm) Nov–Feb: 10am–5:30pm Thu–Sun (last admission 5pm) ■ Adm ■ www. villaemo.org

Another of Palladio's light-flooded country residences, this villa was built for the Emo family in around 1560. A harmonious central block is flanked by graceful arched *barchesse* (wings), designed for storing hay and farm tools. The interior has lively frescoes by Renaissance artist Zelotti, also responsible for the Malcontenta villa decorations.

8 Villa Contarini

Piazzola sul Brenta ■ Open Mar–Oct: 9am–7pm Thu–Tue; Nov–Feb: 10am–4pm Thu–Tue ■ Adm ■ www.villacontarini.eu

A horseshoe plaza lined with terraced houses faces the façade of this 17th-century country villa, which was once the focus for a thriving farming community. A remarkable system of acoustics was invented so that musicians performing in the Sala della Musica on the first floor could be clearly heard and appreciated downstairs. An antiques market is held in the grounds on the last Sunday of each month.

9 Villa Cornaro

Via Roma 35, Piombino Dese ■ Open May–Sep: 3:30–6pm Sat ■ Adm

This unusual, double-tiered creation by Palladio dates to between 1560 and 1570. The façade columns are both Doric and Corinthian in style, with acanthus leaves or scrolls around the capitals. The interior has frescoes by Mattio Borotoloni.

10 Barchessa Valmarana

Via Valmarana 11, Mira ■ Open Apr–Oct: 10am–1pm Tue–Fri (to 4:30pm Sat & Sun; Nov–Mar: to 4:30pm Sat & Sun) ■ Adm ■ www. villavalmarana.net

Formerly guest quarters, these are extant "wings" of a 17th-century villa, whose main body was demolished in 1908. Close by are locks on the Brenta waterway, which have been excavated over centuries to divert the river away from the lagoon and eliminate the problem of silting.

Beautiful interior of Villa Emo

See map on pp128–9

Veneto Shops

① Pasticceria Gelateria Al Duomo
Via Vandelli 2, Padua ■ Closed Tue

This pastry shop has been serving the finest *fritelle* (apple fritters) in town for many decades. It is located on the southern corner of the square by the Duomo.

② Drogheria ai Due Catini d'Oro Dal Zio
Piazza dei Frutti 46, Padua
■ Closed Sun

Strong mints, peppery Veneto *mostarda* chutney and even feather dusters, among many other things, are sold at this old-fashioned shop.

③ Lo Scarabocchio Di Cestari Arrigo
Via Ponte Pietra 25, Verona
■ Closed Sun

A contemporary boutique featuring artisanal clothing and accessories.

④ Antica Pasticceria di Sorarù
Piazzetta Palladio 17, Vicenza

This pastry shop is lined with almond and chocolate delicacies, as well as special goodies such as the dove-shaped *colomba* cake at Easter.

Antica Pasticceria di Sorarù

⑤ Cappelleria Palladio
Piazzetta Palladio 13, Vicenza

Run by a charming couple with a 40-year passion for millinery, this charming old-fashioned shop is a hat-lover's heaven. It is in great demand for stylish weddings in the country villas *(see pp132–3)*.

⑥ LaFeltrinelli
Via S Francesco 7, Padua

You could occupy yourself for hours by browsing the well-stocked shelves of crime and mystery novels, fiction, travel, classics, children's literature and reference books in this chain bookshop.

⑦ Il Ceppo
Corso Palladio 196, Vicenza
■ Closed Sun

A gourmet's paradise, Il Ceppo has mouthwatering takeaway dishes, pickles and preserves. Buy a catered picnic with wine or simply a crusty roll filled with Asiago cheese or *sopressa* sausage.

⑧ De Rossi "Il Fornaio"
Corso Porta Borsari 3, Verona
■ Closed Mon

A range of pastries and wholemeal breads is available here. Try the *zaletto* (a biscuit baked with pine nuts and sultanas), and of course *Baci di Giulietta* (Juliet's Kisses) – almond paste shaped into pursed lips.

⑨ Mercante d'Oriente
Corso Sant'Anastasia 34, Verona ■ Closed Mon & Sun

Akin to a museum, this antiques dealer dazzles with Chinese and Japanese marvels, Pre-Columbian pieces and traditional and contemporary carpets.

⑩ Coin
Via Cappello 30, Verona

This wonderful department store with a good range of casual clothes, cosmetics and home furnishings is right in the centre of town.

Places to Eat

PRICE CATEGORIES

For a three-course meal for one with half a bottle of wine (or equivalent meal), taxes and extra charges.

€ under €40 €€ €40–60 €€€ over €60

① Graziati
Piazza della Frutta 40, Padua
■ 049 875 10 14 ■ Closed Wed ■ €

Light and buttery *millefoglie* pastries perfectly accompany the strong, sweet coffee as you sit outside on the lively market square. Light lunches are served downstairs.

② Caffè Pedrocchi
Via VIII Febbraio 15, Padua
■ 049 878 12 31 ■ €

This 1831 Neo-Classical coffee house was long known as the "café without doors" because it never closed. Liberals of the 19th century would often meet and argue here.

Decor at Caffè Pedrocchi

③ Osteria dei Fabbri
Via dei Fabbri 13, Padua ■ 049 650 336 ■ Closed Sun dinner ■ €

The appetizing menu at this rustic *osteria* changes daily. Typical dishes include grilled Piedmont cheese with polenta or spare ribs with chicory.

④ Antico Guelfo
Contrà Pedemuro San Biagio 90, Vicenza ■ 044 454 78 97
■ Closed Tue ■ €€

This central, upmarket restaurant offers more than the usual fare, including superb gluten-free cuisine. It also has an excellent selection of wines. It offers great value for price.

⑤ Antica Casa della Malvasia
Contrà delle Morette 5, Vicenza
■ 044 454 37 04 ■ Closed Sun dinner, Mon, 2 weeks in Jul ■ €

There is an imaginative menu and vast wine list here. Try the *bigoli all'arna* (spaghetti with duck sauce).

⑥ Bar Borsa
Piazza dei Signori 26, Vicenza
■ 044 454 45 83 ■ Closed Mon–Fri lunch ■ €

With live music and DJs, hip Borsa attracts a lively crowd. Outdoor seating is on Piazza dei Signori as well as Piazza delle Erbe. It has an all-day menu and offers brunch at weekends.

⑦ Angolo Palladio
Piazzetta Palladio 12, Vicenza
■ 044 432 77 90 ■ Closed Mon–Fri lunch ■ €€

This warm and friendly pizzeria-cum-restaurant serves excellent *baccalà* (salt cod) and features an extensive wine list.

⑧ Ristorante Greppia
Vicolo Samaritana 3, Verona
■ 045 800 45 77 ■ Closed Mon, 1–15 Jun ■ €

The unforgettable Greppia specializes in *bollito misto*, a selection of nine melt-in-the-mouth meats served with peppery *Pearà* sauce.

⑨ Arche
Via Arche Scaligere 6, Verona
■ 045 800 74 15 ■ Closed Mon, Sun dinner, 2 weeks in Jan ■ €–€€€

Established in 1879, this is one of the best restaurants in Verona. Fish dishes feature strongly on the menu.

⑩ Bottega del Vino
Vicolo Scudo di Francia 3, Verona ■ 045 800 45 35 ■ €€

Dating from 1890, this renowned restaurant holds 2,500 wines in its cellar. The favourite dish among aficionados is *pastissada de caval*, a dark, spicy horse-meat stew.

See map on pp128–9

Streetsmart

Colourful canal houses on Burano

Getting Around

Arriving by Air

The main international airport, **Aeroporto di Venezia Marco Polo** (Venice Marco Polo Airport) is located 10 km (6.5 miles) north of the city. It is served by many European airlines, such as **British Airways** and low-cost carriers **easyJet** and **Jet2**, and the national carrier **ITA Airways**. London, Frankfurt, Amsterdam and Paris are also transport hubs for Venice. From the US, **Delta Airlines** departs from New York, and **American Airlines** flies direct from Philadelphia.

To transfer to the city from Marco Polo Airport, you can travel by bus, airport shuttle or taxi, but the most exciting way to reach Venice from the airport is by water. The public **Alilaguna** water bus (*vaporetto*) leaves every 15 minutes and takes about an hour. Tickets (€15) are available at the nearby quayside. A water taxi (*motoscafo*) takes about half the time but will cost around €110. The cheaper option is to take a bus to Piazzale Roma. The direct **ATVO Airport bus** (€8) and the **ACTV public bus** No. 5 (€8) leave every 30 minutes. There is a ticket office in the arrivals hall.

Charter flights and low-cost airline **Ryanair** also fly into **Antonio Canova Airport** at Treviso, which is 40 km (29 miles) northwest of Venice. To reach Venice from here, take an ATVO Airport Bus to Piazzale Roma (€10), which takes around 50 minutes, or the public bus No. 6 (€1.30) to Treviso station and then continue by train.

For those visiting the Veneto, Valerio Catullo Airport, in Verona, receives direct flights from the UK, other European countries and Africa. A bus service connects to Verona city centre, and costs around €5 each way. In summer a direct minibus shuttles visitors to Lake Garda.

International Train Travel

Italy's train network is operated by **Trenitalia**. Regular high-speed trains connect the main towns and cities of the Veneto to the rest of Italy, Austria, Germany, France and countries in Eastern Europe. Reservations for these services are essential, and tickets get booked up quickly.

Train Travel in Venice and the Veneto

The easiest and most convenient way to get around the Veneto from Venice is by rail. Trenitalia runs an extensive and efficient network throughout the region, and the cost of travel is very reasonable. Services range from the slow *regionale,* which stops at every station en route, through the various intercity trains to the high-speed Freccia and Eurostar, which link Venice with Verona

Porta Nuova and beyond. Direct lines serve **Venezia Santa Lucia** – Venice's main railway station – and **Venezia Mestre** from numerous northern Italian towns including Bologna, Florence, Milan and Verona. Both stations are extremely busy, with over 450 trains arriving in Venice daily.

Train tickets must be validated before boarding by stamping them in machines at the entrance to platforms. Heavy fines are levied if you are caught on board with an unvalidated ticket.

Long-Distance Bus Travel

An inexpensive way to travel to Venice is by coach. **SITA Bus** offers reasonably priced coach travel throughout Italy. You can buy tickets on board, and services usually depart from outside main railway stations or from the main piazza of smaller towns or cities.

FlixBus is a low-cost intercity coach network with direct services to Venice from Florence, Milan, Naples, Rome and Turin, as well as from international destinations. Coaches into Venice arrive at the main bus terminus in Piazzale Roma.

Cruise Travel

Venice is one of the busiest cruise ports in the Mediterranean, with around 500 ships per year and over 700,000 cruise passengers. The city has two main cruise basins, Marittima (near the main Santa Lucia railway station) for large vessels, and San Basilio (in Giudecca canal) for smaller ships. Both passenger terminals are managed by the **Venezia Terminal Passeggeri**. An automated People Mover carries passengers from the central part of the terminal to Piazzale Roma in minutes. However, it is usually more convenient to travel by the shuttle buses that are provided by the individual cruise companies as they pull up at boarding points. Santa Marta and San Basilio are served by vaporetto line 6, which terminates at the Lido.

If you do choose to arrive in Venice by cruise ship, it's important to be aware of the issues that surround this increasingly popular mode of transport, and the detrimental effects it is having on the city and its lagoon. Venetians have a complicated relationship with cruising vessels. Although they do provide local jobs, the average cruise liner emits as much pollution as 14,000 cars, damages the already fragile lagoon environment and brings in an unmanageable number of visitors to this tiny city. While their plight is often overlooked by the Italian government, the *No Grandi Navi* (no big ships) campaign – which calls to ban large cruise ships entering the lagoon – is gaining significant attention on the global stage. Their cause has even been taken up by UNESCO, who have threatened to put Venice and its lagoon on their list of endangered heritage sites unless the ban on cruise ships goes ahead.

Public Transport

Each city in the Veneto has its own public transport provider. Safety and hygiene measures, timetables, ticket information, transport maps, and more can be obtained from their individual websites.

Verona is served by **ATV**, Padua by **APS Holding**, Vicenza by **AIM Mobilità** and Belluno and the surrounding area by **Dolimiti Bus**.

Venice has a unique transport system. No cars, buses or bicycles are allowed in the streets, and boats are the city's main mode of transportation. Venice's transit authority, the **ACTV**, operates three different types of waterbus – *vaporetti*, *motoscafi* and *motonavi* – plus a network of buses on the Lido and the mainland.

Waterbus

Vaporetti are the slow, single-storey waterbuses you will see chugging along the major canals. They are flat-decked and fully accessible for wheelchairs, prams and buggies, with plenty of seating and standing room. The most popular route is line 1, which makes a leisurely journey down the Grand Canal from Piazzale Roma to San Marco. Faster, more streamlined *moto-scafi* travel beyond the sheltered waters of the city to outlying islands, as do the large double-decker *motonavi* ferries.

Waterbus stops are shown on most Venice maps and are clearly signposted around the city. Their yellow and white floating platforms are easy to spot. At stops with multiple platforms, check the boat number you require and the direction of travel. All the departure quays (*pontile*) have route maps and timetables.

Tickets are available from ACTV booths, from machines at larger stops and also at some newsstands and tobacconists. Validate your ticket at the white electronic ticket reader near the entrance to the platform prior to boarding. Note that green ticket readers are "read only" and will not validate your ticket. If the stop doesn't have a ticket machine, you can approach the conductor immediately after embarkation and ask for a *biglietto*. If you are caught travelling without a validated ticket, you may be fined.

Gondola Traghetto

These are large unadorned gondolas which cross the canal at seven points between San Marco and the railway station from early morning until around 7 or 8pm (although they are not all always in operation). They are rowed by oarsmen who ply backwards and forwards with no fixed timetable, and are a fun and convenient way of crossing the Grand Canal, as it only has four bridges. Simply wait on a *traghetto* pier for the boat to arrive. Pay cash (€2 per person) to the oarsman as you board or leave the gondola. It is customary to stand up for the crossing, but you can opt to sit if you prefer. (Note that these vessels are not suitable for wheelchair users. Instead, travel one stop on vaporetto Line 1 to cross, as it conveniently zigzags the length of the Grand Canal.)

Gondola

Venice's traditional hand-built wooden gondolas are undoubtedly the most romantic way to see the city, but also the most expensive, used almost exclusively by tourists. There are a number of gondola ranks along the Grand Canal, including beside the Palazzo Ducale and Rialto, and also at busy pedestrian crossings along secondary canals. Each location offers a different type of gondola experience – choose whether you would prefer to experience the hustle and bustle of the Grand Canal or a quieter backwater before you

start. Official tariffs should be available at the dock. Expect to pay around €80 for the first 40 minutes, then €40 for additional 20-minute increments. After 7pm, prices are hiked to around €100, and €50 for an extra 20 minutes. However, do not assume you will automatically pay the going rate: before boarding, agree a price with the gondolier to avoid being overcharged. Most gondoliers speak English and have a good knowledge of the main Venetian sights, art and history.

Water Taxi

Small, sleek motorboats, with highly polished wooden decking and stylish leather-upholstered cabins comprise Venice's water taxi fleet – an elite form of transport, which is reflected in the price. Expect to pay around €50–70 for a short hop within the city; and in excess of €110 to travel from the airport to a city centre abode. Water taxis can hold up to ten people, making it a viable option if you are splitting the fare with family or friends.

Bus

In Venice, buses serve the mainland and the Lido only. The main bus station in Venice is at Piazzale Roma near the main train station. On the Lido, route A serves the north of the island, while route B heads south.

City buses in the Veneto are cheap and regular. Tickets, which must be bought prior to travel, are available from newsstands, tobacconists, and shops that display the relevant bus company logo in the window. A flat fee usually covers the city centre and suburbs. Tickets must be validated upon boarding.

People Mover

This high-tech elevated People Mover tramway shuttles passengers cheaply and rapidly between the city's three main arrival points: Marittima cruise terminal, the Tronchetto parking island and Piazzale Roma. It runs 7am to 11pm Monday to Saturday, 8am to 10pm (9pm in winter) on Sundays and costs €1.50. Tickets are available at all three stations. You must scan your ticket to validate it at ground level before you can access the tramway.

Walking

Although it is very pleasant to sit on a vaporetto as you cruise down the Grand Canal or visit the outlying islands on one of the big *moto-navi* ferries, Venice is a tiny city and all the main sights in the *centro storico* are accessible on foot within half-an-hour of each other.

It is also a city where getting lost in the tangle of alleyways *(calli)* is part of the attraction. Take the time to explore these backwaters, with their hidden churches, monuments, squares and locals' bars and restaurants, for a taste of hidden Venice.

Just remember to follow the frequent yellow signs on the walls indicating the direction of the main sights, keep to the right and keep moving on bridges or in the narrowest alleyways.

Bicycle Hire

Cycling is not allowed in Venice city centre, but bike hire is popular on the mainland and on some of the islands in the lagoon, including the Lido. The **RideMovi** city bicycle scheme has a number of stations for bike hire in Marghera and Mestre, and three on the Lido (at Piazzale Santa Maria Elisabetta; Palazzo del Cinema/Via Candia; and Riva di Giovanni Diacono/Piazzale Malamocco). The first half an hour is free, the second half costs €0.50, the following hour €1, and then it's €2 per hour thereafter.

Car Rental

There are a number of car rental offices at Marco Polo, Treviso Antonio Canova and Valerio Catullo airports and at Piazzale Roma, including **Avis**, **Europcar** and **Hertz**, for those wishing to explore the Veneto. Some of the smaller towns and scenic drives are only accessible by private vehicle, and the rolling hills of the Veneto landscape make it perfect terrain for a scenic driving holiday.

To rent a car you must be over 21 and have held a valid driver's licence for at least a year. Driving licences issued by any of the EU member states are valid throughout

the European Union, including Italy. If visiting from outside the EU, you may need to apply for an International Driving Permit.

Rules of the Road

Drive on the right, use the left lane only for passing, and yield to traffic from the right. Seat belts are required for all passengers, and heavy fines are levied for using a mobile phone while driving. A strict drink-drive limit is enforced. During the day dipped headlights are compulsory when you are driving on motorways, dual carriageways and on all out-of-town roads. A red warning triangle, spare tyre and fluorescent vests must be carried for use in an emergency. In the event of an accident or breakdown, switch on your hazard warning lights and place the warning triangle 50 m (55 yd) behind your vehicle. For breakdowns, call the ACI emergency number (116) or the emergency services. The ACI will tow any foreign-registered vehicle to the nearest ACI-affiliated garage free of charge.

DIRECTORY

BICYCLE HIRE

RideMovi
W ridemovi.com

CAR RENTAL

Avis
W avis.com

Europcar
W europcar.com

Hertz
W hertz.com

Practical Information

Passports and Visas

For entry requirements, including visas, consult the nearest Italian embassy or check the **Polizia di Stato** website. All visitors to Italy need a valid passport. Citizens of the UK, US, Canada, Australia and New Zealand do not need a visa for stays of up to three months but, from late 2023, must apply in advance for the European Travel Information and Authorization System (**ETIAS**). Visitors from other countries may also require an ETIAS, so check before travelling. EU nationals do not need a visa or an ETIAS.

Government Advice

It is important to consult both your and the Italian government's advice before travelling. The **UK Foreign, Commonwealth and Developement Office (FCDO)**, the **US Department of State**,the **Australian Department of Foreign Affairs and Trade** and the Italian **Ministero della Salute** offer the latest information on security, health and local regulations.

Customs Information

You can find information on the laws relating to goods and currency taken in or out of Italy on the **ENIT** (Italy's national tourist board) website. Allowances for visitors from the EU are almost unlimited. If you need medication, bring enough and keep a copy of your prescription.

Insurance

We recommend that you take out a comprehensive insurance policy covering theft, loss of belongings, medical care, cancellations and delays, and read the small print carefully.

UK and EU citizens are eligible for free emergency medical care in Italy provided they have a valid EHIC (European Health Insurance Card) or UK **GHIC** (Global Health Insurance Card). Australia has a reciprocal health care agreement with Italy and citizens can access essential medical treatment as long as they are registered to **Medicare**.

Health

Italy has a world-class healthcare system. Emergency medical care in Italy is free for all UK, EU and Australian citizens. If you have an EHIC or GHIC, be sure to present this as soon as possible. You may have to pay after treatment and reclaim the money later.

For other visitors, the payment of medical expenses is the patient's responsibility. Hence, it is important to arrange comprehensive medical insurance.

The **Health Venice** website lists doctors and pharmacies, and tourist offices provide details for night doctors and dentists. Seek medical supplies and advice for minor ailments from pharmacies *(farmacie)*. A rota *(farmacie di turno)* of night-time

and Sunday opening is posted online and on pharmacy doors.

No inoculations are needed to travel to Italy. It is safe to drink tap water and water from fountains unless you see the sign *non potabile* (not drinkable).

Smoking, Alcohol and Drugs

Smoking is banned in enclosed public places and the possession of illegal drugs is prohibited and could result in a prison sentence.

Italy has a strict limit of 0.05 per cent BAC (blood alcohol content) for drivers. This means that you cannot drink more than a small beer or a small glass of wine if you plan to drive. For drivers with less than three years' driving experience, and those under 21, the limit is 0.

ID

By law you must carry identification at all times in Italy. A photocopy of your passport photo page (and visa if applicable) should suffice. If stopped by the police you may be asked to present the original document within 12 hours.

Personal Security

Italy is relatively safe, and even in a city like Venice street violence is rare. The historic centre is well policed, but pickpocketing is common. Leave important documents and valuables in a safe place and only carry the money you need. Be extra vigilant at train stations, markets, on public transport and at the landing stages of the *vaporetti,* especially while boarding.

Dial 112 for a **general emergency** – the operator will ask which service you require. For **ambulance** emergencies you can also dial 118; for the **fire brigade** the direct number is 115.

There are two police forces, the **Carabinieri**, the military branch, and the **Polizia di Stato**, the civil branch. They fulfill much the same functions. Crimes can be reported to either, and both can issue the crime or loss reports *(denuncia di furto o smarrimento)* that you will need when making an insurance claim.

Contact your embassy if you have your passport stolen, or in the event of a serious crime or accident.

As a rule, Venetians are very accepting of all people, regardless of their race, gender or sexuality. Homosexuality was legalized in 1887 and in 1982, Italy became the third country to recognise the right to legally change your gender. If you do feel unsafe, the **Safe Space Alliance** pinpoints your nearest place of refuge.

Women may receive unwanted and unwelcome attention, especially around tourist areas. If you feel threatened, head straight for the nearest police station.

Travellers with Specific Requirements

Venice has made real effort to improve access for travellers with specific requirements, with 70 per cent of the centre now accessible to those with impaired mobility and most sites reachable by public transport. However, many older buildings do not have wheelchair access or lifts.

Some city museums offer free admission to disabled people and carers, as well as induction loops and audio guides for the hearing impaired and partially sighted. Many of the city's bridges are fitted with low steps but no stair lifts, while all vaporetto stops are accessible for people with impaired mobility. The main routes can carry up to four wheelchairs and a discounted disabled ticket costs €1.50 including a carer.

The Venezia Accessibile information pack on the **Sanitrans** website lists barrier-free itineraries, accessible public toilets, and travel arrangements, including manageable bridges. It also lists shops where you can hire wheelchairs. The **Comune di Venezia** website also includes itineraries designed for travellers with disabilities, as well as a map of accessible Venice, and the **Sage Travel** website is packed with detailed information. **Enable Holidays** specializes in tailor-made packages.

DIRECTORY

PASSPORTS AND VISAS

ETIAS
w etiasvisa.com

Polizia di Stato
w poliziadistato.it

GOVERNMENT ADVICE

Australian Department of Foreign Affairs and Trade
w smartraveller.gov.au

Ministero della Salute
w salute.gov.it

UK Foreign, Commonwealth and Development Office
w gov.uk/foreign-travel-advice

US Department of State
w travel.state.gov

CUSTOMS INFORMATION

ENIT
w italia.it

INSURANCE

GHIC
w ghic.org.uk

Medicare
w humanservices.gov.au

HEALTH

Health Venice
w healthvenice.com

PERSONAL SECURITY

Ambulance
c 118

Carabinieri
c 112
w carabinieri.it

Fire Brigade
c 115

General Emergency
c 112

Polizia di Stato
c 113

Safe Space Alliance
w safespacealliance.com

TRAVELLERS WITH SPECIFIC REQUIREMENTS

Enable Holidays
w enableholidays.com

Comune di Venezia
w comunevenezia.it

Sage Travel
w sagetraveling.com

Sanitrans
w sanitrans.netlde

Time Zone

Italy operates on Central European Time (CET), which is one hour ahead of Greenwich Mean Time (GMT). The clock moves forward one hour during daylight saving time from the last Sunday in March to the last Sunday in October.

Money

Italy is one of the many European countries using the euro (€). Most establishments accept major credit, debit and prepaid currency cards.

Contactless payments are becoming increasingly common in Venice, but it's always a good idea to carry some cash for smaller items such as coffee, gelato and pizza-by-the-slice. Cash is also needed to use public toilets and ticket machines at stations.

Wait staff should be tipped €1–2 and hotel porters and housekeeping will expect €1 per bag or day.

Electrical Appliances

In Italy, standard voltage is 220–230 volts. Power sockets are type F and L, fitting plugs with two and three round-pronged pins. Appliances with non-Italian plugs will need adaptors.

Mobile Phones and Wi-Fi

Wi-Fi is widely available throughout Venice, and cafés and restaurants will usually give you the password for their Wi-Fi on the condition that you make a purchase. Much of the city has wireless hotspots. You can buy access to the municipal Venice Wi-Fi network, which operates mostly on the main squares and thoroughfares, for 24 hours, 72 hours or a week through the **Venezia Unica** city pass.

Visitors travelling to Italy with EU tariffs are able to use their devices abroad without being affected by roaming charges. Users will be charged the same rates for data, SMS and voice calls as they would pay at home. Visitors from other countries, with unlocked mobile phones, can buy an Italian pay-as-you-go SIM card from **TIM**, **Wind** or **Vodafone**. Top-ups are available from tobacconists (tabacchi) and newsstands.

Postal Services

Main post offices are found in the Rialto and on the Piazzale Roma. Stamps (francobolli) can be bought at post offices and tabacchi, which are recognizable by the black-and-white "T" sign. You can find a complete list of post offices on the **Poste Italiane** website.

Weather

Every season in Venice has its attractions, but July and August can get very hot (up to 30° C/ 86° F) and sticky. Between October and March, Venice often experiences acqua alta (tidal flooding), which spreads out from Piazza San Marco. Sirens give an alert to an impending flood, and a network of passerelle (wooden walk-ways) are erected on the main routes around the city. Visitors should come prepared with boots or overshoes. Check the weather forecast on **Il Meteo**. You can find tide height information on the **Città di Venezia** website or its hi!tide Venice app.

Opening Hours

Many museums are open daily, however, the times are subject to change, so it is wise to check ahead. The main churches are usually open 10am–5pm Monday to Saturday. Food shops are open 9am–1pm and 4–7.30pm Monday to Saturday, except for Wednesday afternoon. In low season, many stores close all day Sunday and also Monday mornings.

The COVID-19 pandemic proved that situations can change suddenly. Always check before visiting attractions and hospitality venues for up-to-date hours and booking requirements.

Visitor Information

Venice tourist office, **Venezia Unica**, offers a range of discount cards to make visiting Venice easier on the purse strings. These passes give access to public toilets, Wi-Fi, museums, churches and vaporetti. For young people aged 16-29 years, the €6 Rolling Venice pass and

ACTV 3 Day Youth Pass entitle discounted travel and reduced admission to a number of sights.

Students should bring an **International Student Identity Card (ISIC)** with them for reduced fares and entry fees.

Senior travellers are also eligible for reduced fees to churches and museums, with a photographic ID as proof of age. If travelling by train, it's best to buy the *carta d'argento*, which gives over-60s a 15 per cent discount. The card is available at stations, travel agencies or online.

The **Museum Pass** (€40) allows entry to 12 museums. If you intend visiting a number of churches, consider a **Chorus Pass** (€12), which gives entry to 16 churches and organizes guided tours (single entrance to churches costs €3).

Responsible Tourism

In response to the high volume of tourists visiting Venice, the **#Enjoy-RespectVenezia** campaign was launched in 2017 to raise awareness of tourist impact and to encourage responsible tourism in the city. The campaign asks that visitors follow certain rules to lessen their impact: walk on the right, do not linger on busy bridges, do not cycle in the city or lead bikes by hand. The steps of churches, bridges, wells, monuments and canalbanks are not picnic areas, nor are squares or *campi* – instead head to public gardens. Do not

jump into the canals or attempt to swim in the lagoon, except at designated spots. Do not wear inappropriate clothing such as swimwear in the city. Don't drop litter – instead dispose of waste properly and recycle wherever possible. Do not feed pigeons, and respect the privacy of local residents.

Camping is also prohibited in the city, as is attaching padlocks to buildings or bridges, or buying fake goods from illegal street vendors.

Language

Italian is the official language, though many people speak a Venetian dialect. English is widely spoken.

Taxes and Refunds

VAT (called IVA in Italy) is usually 22 per cent, with a reduced rate of 4–10 per cent on some items. Non-EU citizens can claim an IVA rebate.

Accommodation

Venice's hotels cater for every budget. Hotels nearest Piazza San Marco are the most expensive, and a view of a canal costs more. For those visiting Venice on a budget, consider staying in Mestre, or on the Lido across the lagoon. It's wise to book as far ahead as you can and to look for special deals online. Spaces fill up quickly at Carnival time, Easter, from June to September, and over Christmas and New Year.

Hotels throughout Italy charge overnight guests a tourist tax *(imposta di soggiorno)* on top of room price. Under Italian law, hotels are required to register guests at police headquarters and issue a receipt of payment *(ricevuta fiscale)*, which you must keep until you leave Italy.

Places to Stay

Luxury Hotels

Grand Hotel Palazzo dei Dogi

MAP D1 ■ Fondamenta Madonna dell'Orto, Cannaregio 3500 ■ 041 220 81 11 ■ www. nh-hotels.com ■ €€

On a quiet Cannaregio canal, with a lovely garden stretching back to the lagoon, this former convent is furnished with Murano chandeliers and fabrics crafted by leading artisans. This is the best-value luxury hotel in town, and has its own guest launch.

Aman Venice

MAP N3 ■ San Polo 1364 ■ 041 270 73 33 ■ www. aman.com ■ €€€

The hotel launch brings guests from the airport to the Grand Canal entrance of Palazzo Papadopoli. You step straight into the original palace, with its stuccoed rooms, as well as a small spa and a gym. The hotel also has spacious common rooms and lovely gardens.

Al Ponte Antico

MAP P3 ■ Calle dell' Aseo, Cannareggio 5768 ■ 041 241 19 44 ■ www. alponteantico.com ■ €€€

A hotel based in a 5th-century Venetian palace with magnificent interiors. Breakfast and *aperitivo* are served in the small terrace overlooking the Canal Grande.

Excelsior Venice Lido Resort

MAP H2 ■ Lungomare Marconi 41, Lido ■ 041 526 02 01 ■ Closed Nov–mid-Mar ■ www.hotel excelsiorvenezia.com ■ €€€

Crawling with stars during the Film Festival, this hotel has rooms right on the beach. There is also a swimming pool and exclusive restaurants.

Hotel Cipriani

MAP E6 ■ Giudecca 10 ■ 041 520 77 44 ■ www.hotelcipriani.com ■ Closed Nov–Mar ■ €€€

Set on Giudecca, Cipriani is just minutes from the water. It has a private garden with a salt-water pool, and three top restaurants *(see p64)*.

Hotel Danieli

MAP R5 ■ Riva degli Schiavoni, Castello 4196 ■ 041 522 64 80 ■ www. danielihotelvenice.com ■ €€€

Set in a pink palazzo, Danieli has a long history of famous guests *(see p109)*. The hotel is close to the Bridge of Sighs and Piazza San Marco.

JW Marriott Venice Resort

MAP N4 ■ Isole delle Rose, Venice Lagoon ■ 041 852 13 00 ■ Closed Nov–Feb ■ www.jwvenice.com ■ €€€

In parkland on an island in the Southern Lagoon, this resort offers suites, roof terraces, swimming pools, a spa and a choice of restaurants, as well as daily cooking classes. The private shuttle launch takes 20 minutes to reach Piazza San Marco.

Luna Hotel Baglioni

MAP P5 ■ Calle Larga dell'Ascension, S Marco 1243 ■ 041 240 00 01 ■ www.baglionihotels. com ■ €€€

Enjoy exquisite service in a refined atmosphere of chandeliers and marble. This is Venice's oldest hotel – it hosted the Knights Templar in the 1100s, while they waited to embark for the Crusades. Breakfast is served in the drawing room, frescoed by pupils of Tiepolo.

Metropole

MAP F4 ■ Riva degli Schiavoni, Castello 4149 ■ 041 520 50 44 ■ www. hotelmetropole.com ■ €€€

This good-value, grand establishment is immaculately run. On the waterfront, minutes from San Marco, it has a wonderful garden and a Michelin-starred restaurant.

Palace Bonvecchiati

MAP Q4 ■ Calle dei Fabbri, S Marco 4680 ■ 041 296 31 11 ■ www. palacebonvecchiati.it ■ €€€

"Contemporary luxury" best describes this hotel with a roof-level sauna and gym. Private canal access means guests can arrive by water taxi.

St Regis Venice Hotel
MAP P6 ▪ Corte Barozzi, S Marco 2159 ▪ 041 240 00 01 ▪ www.marriot.it ▪ €€€
This elegant historic palace, on the Grand Canal, is beautifully decorated. It is also quite close to the Piazza San Marco.

Budget Hotels

Al Campaniel Guesthouse
MAP L4 ▪ Calle del Campaniel, S Polo 2889 ▪ 041 275 07 49 ▪ €
Spanish-Venetian couple Gloria and Marco are discreet and professional hosts offering spotless rooms close to the San Tomà boat stop. Each room has tea- and coffee-making facilities.

Alloggi Gerotto Calderan
MAP C2 ▪ Campo S Geremia, Cannaregio 283 ▪ 041 715 361 ▪ Closed Christmas week ▪ No credit cards ▪ www.alloggi-gerotto-calderan-venice-it. hotelmix.it ▪ €
Handy for the station, this hotel has airy rooms, some with bath (no breakfast). Guests are welcomed by enthusiastic English-speaking staff. Try to bargain down the rates in low season.

Al Santo
Via del Santo 147, Padua ▪ 049 875 21 31 ▪ Closed 7–30 Jan ▪ www.alsanto.it ▪ €
This simple family-run hotel is very well located, 10 minutes' stroll from Padua's main historic sights (see p129).

Bernardi Semenzato
MAP P1 ▪ Calle dell'Oca, Cannaregio 4366 ▪ 041 522 72 57 ▪ www.hotel bernardi.com ▪ €
Located near Campo dei Santi Apostoli, this hotel is a delightful bargain. The owners are extremely hospitable.

Casa Cardinal Piazza
MAP D1 ▪ Fondamenta Contarini, Cannaregio 3539/A ▪ 041 720 233 ▪ No credit cards ▪ www.casacardinal piazza.org ▪ €
Run by friendly nuns, this great-value palace guesthouse is set in a shady garden right on the lagoon edge. It has 24 modest rooms, all of which have en-suite bathrooms. Breakfast is available; there's an 11pm curfew.

Hotel Gobbo
MAP C2 ▪ Campo S Geremia 312, Cannaregio ▪ 041 715 001 ▪ www. albergoalgobbo.it ▪ €
The "Hunchback" is a clean, small-scale hotel. Most of the rooms have air conditioning, and a couple overlook a bustling square. Easy access from the railway station.

Istituto Canossiano
MAP K6 ▪ Fondamenta de le Romite, Dorsoduro 1323 ▪ 041 240 97 11 ▪ Closed Christmas week, 2 weeks in Aug ▪ No air conditioning ▪ www. romite1323.com ▪ €
This modernized, and converted convent has vast courtyards to wander around. Vending machines are on hand for snacks and drinks; otherwise, it's not far to the Zattere. Guests should note that there's a midnight curfew.

Il Lato Azzurro
MAP H2 ▪ Via Forti 13, Sant'Erasmo ▪ 041 523 06 42 ▪ No air conditioning ▪ www. latoazzurro.it ▪ €
Il Lato Azzurro offers great-value lodgings on this garden island, where sea breezes are ensured. The hosts can arrange canoe trips, use of bicycles, picnic lunches and half-board, consisting mainly of vegetarian meals. The hotel has two rooms specially equipped for travellers with specific needs.

San Giorgio Monastery
MAP F5 ▪ Isola di San Giorgio Maggiore ▪ 041 241 47 17 ▪ No credit cards ▪ €
The monks on San Giorgio Island, just across the Canale di San Marco from Piazza San Marco, welcome guests to their peaceful premises. A simple breakfast is provided, and self-catering accommodation is also available. There are superb views of Venice from the square in front of the church.

Hotels with Charm

B&B Ca' Noemi
MAP F1 ▪ Rio Terà 32, Malamocco ▪ 041 242 00 40 ▪ www.canoemi.it ▪ €
This renovated 14th-century building is located on the southern end of the Lido in an old fishing village. The nearby Ca 'del Moro Sporting Club has a swimming pool, tennis and physical fitness facilities. There is easy access to the city and the beach.

Accademia Villa Maraveghe
MAP L6 ■ Fondamenta Bollani, Dorsoduro 1058 ■ 041 521 01 88 ■ www.pensioneaccademia.it ■ €€–€€€

Set near the Accademia (see pp30–31), this beautiful 17th-century villa was formerly the Russian embassy. Breakfast can be enjoyed in the private garden. You need to book well in advance.

Ca' della Corte
MAP B3 ■ Corte Surian, Dorsoduro 3560 ■ 041 715 877 ■ www.cadellacorte.com ■ €€

This charming bed-and-breakfast has spotless rooms that has all the latest equipment, including satellite TV. It is just a short stroll to Piazzale Roma.

La Calcina
MAP D5 ■ Zattere, Dorsoduro 780 ■ 041 520 64 66 ■ www.lacalcina.com ■ €€

In 1877, Ruskin stayed at this guesthouse on the Zattere. The rooms have been modernized since then, but they retain their charm and parquet floors. An exclusive street-level terrace overlooks the Giudecca Canal, while another surveys the rooftops. It is advised to book well in advance for a stay here.

Hotel Flora
MAP P5 ■ Calle Bergamaschi, S Marco 2283/A ■ 041 520 58 44 ■ www.hotelflora.it ■ €€

Though small, the pretty internal courtyard with lush greenery at this 17th-century palazzo is an oasis of calm after the city crowds. The charming rooms are individually decorated. Those on the upper floor offer good views.

Hotel Marconi
MAP P3 ■ Riva del Vin, S Polo 729 ■ 041 522 20 68 ■ www.hotelmarconi.it ■ €€

This popular hotel by Rialto Bridge has outside seating reserved for guests. Rooms are simple but guests are given a warm welcome.

Locanda Cipriani
MAP H1 ■ Piazza S Fosca 29, Torcello ■ 041 730 150 ■ Closed Jan–early Feb ■ www.locandacipriani.com ■ €€

A peaceful, sophisticated hotel on the island of Torcello (see pp36–7), Locanda Cipriani has a list of illustrious past guests, and a famed restaurant overlooking the garden. Guests can explore the island after the day-trippers have left.

Palazzo Abadessa
MAP D2 ■ Calle Priuli, Cannaregio 4011 ■ 041 241 37 84 ■ www.abadessa.com ■ €€–€€€

Murano glass chandeliers and lovely fabrics add to the atmosphere at this palace hotel. There are two specially equipped rooms for travellers with specific needs.

San Simon Ai Due Fanali
MAP K1 ■ Campo S Simeone Grande, S Croce 946/949 ■ 041 718 490 ■ www.aiduefanali.com ■ €€

The rooms at this tastefully renovated former monastery have wooden rafters. Several apartments are available near the Arsenale.

The Gritti Palace
MAP N6 ■ Campo S Maria del Giglio, S Marco 2467 ■ 041 794 611 ■ www.marriot.it ■ €€€

Ernest Hemingway stayed in this 15th-century palace-hotel situated on the Grand Canal. Romantic waterside dining is among its many features.

Converted Palaces

Albergo Guerrato
MAP N2 ■ Calle Drio La Scimia, S Polo 240/A ■ 041 522 71 31 ■ Closed 7–30 Jan ■ www.hotelguerrato.com ■ €

This charming, spacious old hotel at Rialto dates back to 1288 and is full of history. Not all rooms are en suite.

Al Sole
MAP J4 ■ Fondamenta Minotto, S Croce 136 ■ 041 244 03 28 ■ www.alsolehotels.com ■ €€

A beautiful place to stay, convenient for Piazzale Roma, this 16th-century palace, with a huge lobby and a courtyard draped in wisteria, is often used as a film set. Rooms have all mod cons.

Ca' Nigra Lagoon Resort
MAP K1 ■ Campo S Simeon Grande, S Croce 927 ■ 041 524 27 90 ■ www.hotelcanigra.com ■ €€–€€€

Once an ambassador's residence, this palace on the Grand Canal has two delightful shady gardens. The decor is modern, and one room even has a private jacuzzi. The location is handy for the railway and bus stations.

Ca' Pisani
MAP F4 ▪ Rio Terrà Foscarini, Dorsoduro 979A ▪ 041 240 14 11 ▪ www.capisanihotel.it ▪ €€

Converted in 2000, Ca' Pisani has a warm ambience, stunning modern design and all the facilities you could hope for. You may never want to leave this 15th-century palace, conveniently close to the Accademia.

Hotel Santo Stefano
MAP M5 ▪ Campo S Stefano, S Marco 2957 ▪ 041 520 01 66 ▪ www.hotelsantostefanovenezia.com ▪ €€

Guests return to this former monastery watch-tower for its discerning style, maximum comfort (there are Jacuzzis in all the rooms) and enjoy breathtaking views.

Locanda La Corte
MAP F3 ▪ Calle Bressana, Castello 6317 ▪ 041 241 13 00 ▪ www.locandalacorte.it ▪ €€

A relaxing atmosphere prevails at this renovated 16th-century palace. It once served the ambassador from Brescia and is impeccably furnished with period pieces. Breakfast is served in the courtyard.

Locanda San Barnaba
MAP L5 ▪ Calle del Traghetto, Dorsoduro 2785–2786 ▪ 041 241 12 33 ▪ www.locanda-san-barnaba-venezia.venice.hotels-veneto.com ▪ €€

Minutes from the Ca' Rezzonico ferry stop, this quiet, elegant

palace-hotel has original frescoes in many of the rooms, which are named after Goldoni's plays.

San Cassiano – Ca' Favretto
MAP N2 ▪ Calle della Rosa, S Croce 2232 ▪ 041 524 17 68 ▪ www.sancassiano.it ▪ €€

Right on the Grand Canal, but hidden away in the maze of alleyways close to Rialto, you'll find this 16th-century palace which has been converted into a hotel named after a 19th-century artist. It offers elegant, well-equipped rooms with Venetian furnishings.

Ruzzini Palace Hotel
MAP R3 ▪ Campo S Maria Formosa, Castello 5866 ▪ 041 241 04 47 ▪ www.ruzzinipalace.com ▪ €€€

Constructed in the late 16th century, this period residence retains its vast frescoed rooms, monumental staircases and a water entrance. It overlooks a typical Venetian square and is only five minutes from Piazza San Marco.

Hotels in Tranquil Locations

Agriturismo Le Garzette
MAP H2 ▪ Lungomare Alberoni 32, Malamocco, Lido ▪ 041 731 078 ▪ Closed Christmas–Feb ▪ www.legarzette.it ▪ €

This attractive family-run establishment, off the beaten track, has only five rooms and this – along with the superb home cooking – will make you feel as though you are part

of the family. It is located very close to the sea and the lagoon.

Ca' San Marcuola
MAP C2 ▪ Campiello della Chiesa, Cannaregio 1763 ▪ 041 716 048 ▪ Closed Dec–Carnival ▪ www.casanmarcuola.com ▪ €

In a handy location close to the *vaporetto* stop, this unpretentious, but quiet and friendly, guesthouse is well appointed.

Due Mori
Contrà Do Rode 24–26, Vicenza ▪ 044 432 18 86 ▪ Closed 1–15 Aug ▪ No air conditioning ▪ www.hotelduemori.com ▪ €

In a quiet street in Vicenza, close to all the main sights *(see p130)*, the Due Mori has spacious, spotless rooms furnished in old-style dark timber.

Hotel Mercurio
MAP D4 ▪ Calle del Fruttariol, S Marco 2848 ▪ 041 522 09 47 ▪ www.hotelmercurio.com ▪ €

This family-run hotel is exceptionally quiet despite being located right in the historic centre near Piazza San Marco. Each room here has a different view of the lagoon or the surrounding streets.

Villa Ducale
Riviera Martiri della Libertà 75, Dolo ▪ ACTV bus 53 from Piazzale Roma ▪ 041 560 80 20 ▪ www.villaducale.it ▪ €

Halfway between Padua and Venice, this stately residence stands in a lovely private park with statues. The beautiful rooms have the usual facilities plus frescoes and glass chandeliers.

Santa Fosca

MAP D2 ■ Fondamenta Vendramin, Cannaregio 2400 ■ 041 275 01 25 ■ www.hotelcaven dramin.it ■ €€

The comfortable rooms in this cosy 16th-century palazzo just off the Strada Nova are lavishly decorated. Breakfast is served in a period-style room with stained-glass windows.

Hotel Falier

MAP K4 ■ Salizzada S Pantalon, S Croce 130 ■ 041 710 882 ■ www. hotelfalier.com ■ €€

This cheery hotel is named after the beheaded traitor Doge Falier, "as a warning to guests who fail to pay!" Sunlight streams into the comfortable, if small, rooms, all of which have an en-suite shower. There's a courtyard dripping with wisteria.

Hotel Giudecca

MAP C6 ■ Corte Ferrando 409 C, Giudecca ■ 041 296 01 68 ■ www.hotel giudeccavenezia.it ■ €€

Located away from the hustle and bustle of the centre, but well-served by public transport, this elegant hotel has 30 rooms and welcomes four-legged friends. Breakfast is included.

Locanda Fiorita

MAP M5 ■ Campiello Novo o dei Morti, S Marco 3457/A ■ 041 523 47 54 ■ www.locandafiorita.com ■ €€

The pretty Locanda Fiorita is located on a sunny square that was once a public cemetery off Campo San Stefano. In spring and summer, enjoy a leisurely breakfast out-side. You can bargain for cheaper rooms in low season.

Medium-Priced Hotels

Al Gallion

MAP K2 ■ Calle Gallion, S Croce 1126 ■ 348 814 15 76 ■ No credit cards ■ No air conditioning ■ www.algallion.com ■ €

Guests are given a warm welcome and insider infor-mation at this small B&B. It is handy for Piazzale Roma and the Riva di Biasio vaporetto stop on the Grand Canal.

Al Saor

MAP P1 ■ Calle Zotti, Cannaregio 3904/A ■ 041 296 06 54 ■ www. alsaor.com ■ €

The owners of this family-run hotel, close to the Ca' d'Oro, offer personal touches: a ride in their own boat for guests, and homemade biscuits for breakfast.

Hotel Torcolo

Vicolo Listone 3, Verona ■ Bus Nos. 11, 12, 13, 51 (or 90, 92, 93 evenings & hols) from Marciapiede A ■ 045 800 75 12 ■ Closed Christmas week ■ www. hoteltorcolo.it ■ €

Just around the corner from the Arena, this hotel is run by a very friendly team. Guest parking is available.

Locanda Ca' Zose

MAP D5 ■ Calle del Bastion, Dorsoduro 197 ■ 041 522 66 35 ■ www. hotelcazose.com ■ €–€€

Rooms are cosy and stylish in this 17th-century building; several have canal views. The hotel is in a very quiet location, handy for La Salute vaporetto and the Peggy Guggenheim Collection.

Rossi

MAP C2 ■ Calle Procuratie, Cannaregio 262 ■ 041 715 562 ■ Closed 6 Jan–6 Feb ■ www.hotel-rossi.all-hotels-venice.com/it ■ €

This popular family-friendly hotel is high on hospitality. Rooms are spotless, and many have lovely views. The hotel is well placed for Strada Nova. Book in advance.

Villa Giustinian

Via Miranese 85, Mirano ■ 041 570 02 00 ■ www. villagiustinian.com ■ €

Housed in an 18th-century villa, this hotel has a swimming pool, park, magnificent rooms and a fine restaurant. Buses run every 20 minutes for the 40-minute trip to Venice.

Al Gambero

MAP P4 ■ Calle dei Fabbri, S Marco 4687 ■ 041 522 43 84 ■ www.locanda algambero.com ■ €€

This old favourite on a bridge halfway between the Rialto and Piazza San Marco is wonderfully located for many sights and shopping sprees. Downstairs is Le Bistrot de Venise, a popular nightspot (see p69).

Al Gazzettino

MAP Q4 ■ Calle di Mezzo, S Marco 4971 ■ 041 528 65 23 ■ www.algazzettino. com ■ €€

Centrally located between the Rialto and San Marco, Al Gazzettino is a basic, decent-value hotel. The downstairs walls are papered with sheets from the city's *Il Gazzettino* newspaper, which was its long-standing neighbour until its relocation to the more practical mainland.

Hotel Novecento

MAP N6 ■ Calle del Dose, Campo S Maurizio, S Marco 2683 ■ 041 241 37 65 ■ www.nove cento.biz ■ €€
The relaxing rooms at this boutique hotel, located halfway between the Accademia and Piazza San Marco, have Orientalist decor, with furniture and tapestries from the Far East. In summer, breakfast is served in the courtyard.

Hostels and Campsites

A&O Venezia Mestre

Via Ca Marcello 19, ■ 041 884 09 90 ■ www. aohostels.com ■ €
Located opposite the Ponte della Libertà, in Mestre, this A&O hostel is six minutes' walking distance from the Venezia-Mestre train station. It offers single, double and dorm rooms, complete with lockers.

Campeggio Miramare

Lungomare D. Alighieri 29, Punta Sabbione ■ 041 966 150 ■ Closed Oct–late Mar ■ www. camping-miramare.it ■ €
One of the many camping grounds at Punta Sabbione on the seaside of Venice, Miramare is linked to the city by ferry (line LN). The camping village has huts and campsites and also offers a range of facilities, including a mini-market and a restaurant-bar.

Camping Fusina

Via Moranzani 93, Fusina ■ 041 547 00 55 ■ www. camping-fusina.com ■ €
This popular three-star venue for campers and backpackers (in a caravan) is right on the lagoon edge. It is well connected via bus No. 11 from Mestre train station or the Alilaguna ferry from the Zattere.

Casa a Colori Padova

Via del Commissario 42, Padova ■ Bus No. 3 ■ 049 680 332 ■ www.casaa coloripadova.org ■ €
The hostel offers various types of accommodation, including single and qua-druple rooms. International breakfast is served daily, and vending machines and Wi-Fi are available in the common areas. The city centre and station are a 15-minute bus ride away.

Foresteria Valdese

MAP R3 ■ Calle Lunga S Maria Formosa, Castello 5170 ■ 041 528 67 97 ■ www.foresteria venezia.it ■ €
This wonderful guesthouse near Campo Santa Maria Formosa *(see p110)* is run by the Waldensian and Methodist community and has frescoed dormi-tories, and two, three and four-bed rooms. Be sure to book in advance.

IYH Ostello Olimpico

Viale Giuriolo 7, Vicenza ■ Bus Nos. 2, 5 or 7 from the railway station ■ 0444 125 00 19 ■ Closed early Nov–Feb ■ www.ostello vicenza.com ■ €
This cheery, helpful hostel is close to the main tourist office and Teatro Olimpico *(see p131)*. Discounts apply at a neighbouring bar and restaurant.

Internet point and bike hire are available.

IYH Ostello Venezia

MAP E6 ■ Fondamenta Zitelle 86, Giudecca ■ 041 877 82 88 ■ www. generatorhostels.com ■ €
This well-run hostel offers inexpensive meals and a lovely setting on Giudecca. It is a 35-minute trip by *vaporetto* from the railway station and 5 minutes by *vaporetto* to Piazza San Marco *(see pp20–23)*.

IYH Ostello Villa Francescatti

Via Santa Chiara 10, Verona ■ Bus No. 73 (Mon–Sat), 91 (evenings & Sun) from the railway station ■ 045 590 360 ■ www.ostellostay generetor.com ■ €
This 16th-century villa on the hillside above the Roman amphitheatre is a youth hostel with dormi-tories. It is 3 km (2 miles) from Verona's train station.

Ostello Santa Fosca

MAP D2 ■ Fondamenta Canal, Cannaregio 2372 ■ 041 715 775 ■ www. ostellosantafosca.it ■ €
Set in rambling convent grounds, this university student hostel lets out dorm beds to back-packers. Cooking facilities are available in summer.

Venezia Camping Village

MAP G1 ■ Via Orlanda 8/C, Mestre ■ 041 531 28 28 ■ Closed early Jan & Feb ■ www.venezia village.it ■ €
With immaculate buildings around and a pool, this site is popular for campers and bungalow rentals. Bus Nos. 5 and 19 take you to Venice in 10 minutes.

For a key to hotel price categories see p146

General Index

Acknowledgments

This edition updated by

Contributor Cristina Minoni
Senior Editor Alison McGill
Senior Designer Vinita Venugopal
Project Editor Tijana Todorinovic
Assistant Editor Ilina Choudhary, Tavleen Kaur
Picture Research Administrator Vagisha Pushp
Manager Picture Research Taiyaba Khatoon
Jacket Designer Jordan Lambley
Senior Cartographer Subhashree Bharati
Cartography Manager Suresh Kumar
Senior DTP Designer Tanveer Zaidi
DTP Designer Rohit Rojal
Senior Production Editor Jason Little
Senior Production Controller Samantha Cross
Managing Editors Shikha Kulkarni, Beverly Smart, Hollie Teague
Managing Art Editor Sarah Snelling
Senior Managing Art Editor Priyanka Thakur
Art Director Maxine Pedliham
Publishing Director Georgina Dee

DK would like to thank the following for their contribution to the previous editions: Charles Hebbert, Kate Hughes, Helen Peters, Gillian Price, Ruth Reisenberger

The publisher would like to thank the following for their kind permission to reproduce their photographs:

Key: a-above; b-below/bottom; c-centre; f-far; l-left; r-right; t-top

4Corners: Luca Da Ros 4t.
Alamy Stock Photo: A.F. Archive 65tr; age fotostock/ Jose Peral 61tl; AGF Srl/Mark Edward Smith 14bl; Alessandro0770 15b; The Art Archive/Collection Dagli Orti 19tl, 23cl; Peter Barritt 27b, 32cla; Bildarchiv Monheim GmbH 36bl; blickwinkel 109br; Paul Carstairs 82c; Frank Chmura 86bl; dpa picture alliance 111bl; Eye Ubiquitous/Paul Seheult 37ca; Peter Erik Forsberg 75clb; funkyfood, London/Paul Williams 10cra; Rik Hamilton 6cla; Hemis.fr /Christian Guy 117bl; Heritage Image Partnership Ltd 55cl, / Fine Art Images 18tl; Oliver Hoffmann 17c; Peter Horree 54b; Image Professionals GmbH / Inga Wandinger 70t; IML Image Group/Roberto Meazza 134bl; Interfoto 51bl, /Fine Arts 51tl; John Warburton-Lee Photography /Ken Scicluna 106clb; John Kellerman 32-3c; Konstantin Kalishko 23b; Roy Kaltschmidt 76b; John Keats 14cra; John Kellerman 17cra, 38–9, 104tl; Alvan Kranzer 51tr; liszt collection/Quint & Lox 53bl; LOOK Die Bildagentur der Fotografen GmbH 12–3c; Dennis MacDonald 111cla; Martin Thomas Photography 114–5; Mary Evans Picture Library 50cb; Thomas Mayer 103br; Moviestore Collection Ltd 53tr; Erick Nguyen 47bl; North Wind Picture Archives 50cla; Sergey Novikov 108ca; Chuck Pefley 35tl; Peter Forsberg 66b; peterforsberg 66cra, 75cla; Ferdinando Piezzi 118tl; Prisma Archivo 52c; Prisma Bildagentur AG/

Sonderegger Christof 59tl; Alex Ramsay 62t; Really Easy Star/Giuseppe Masci 133bl; Reda & Co srl/ Federico Meneghetti 129br; Norbert Scanella 72tr; Matthias Scholz 55tr; TRAVELSCAPES 123tl, 126tl; Unlisted Images, Inc./ Fotosearch 38bl; Peter Vallance 59b; Martyn Vickery 34br; Visions of Serge L 119bl; Ross Warner 37tl, 61b; World History Archive 16cb, 54tl; Zoonar GmbH/Francesco Perre 39bc.
Arnoldo Battois: 84bc.
AWL Images: ClickAlps 1.
Bacarando: 86c.
Osteria Bancogiro: 93ca.
Bevilacqua Tessuti: 85crb.
Signor Blum: 100clb.
Bridgeman Images: Cameraphoto Arte Venezia 19b.
Cesare Sent SNC: 120tc.
Corbis: Alinari Archives/Mauro Magliani 31clb; Atlantide Phototravel/Stefano Amantini 63cr; David Lees 31cla; Sylvain Sonnet 17cl; The Gallery Collection 15cl.
Dorling Kindersley: John Heseltine 44tr, 44b, 45cl
Dreamstime.com: Andreykr 34–5; Antonella865 37bc; Michal Bednarek 24–5; Canonman29 25cra, 82tr, 89tr; Carolannfreeling 46cclb; Marco Clarizia 33tr; Crisferra 58t; Danflcreativo 67br; Dbdella 34clb; Razvan Ionut Dragomirescu 110cla; Viorel Dudau 52tl; Eg004713 128tl; Ekaterinabelova 18br; Emicristea 13tr; Fedecandoniphoto 25br; Inna Felker 47tr; Michael Foley 49tr; Gekkon4ik 26crb; Ihsan Gercelman 6br; Radu Razvan Gheorghe 75tr; Diana Gradeva 116cla; Mark Graham 11ca; Neil Harrison 13cr; Anna Hristova 88cra; Lukasz Janyst 20–21; Wieslaw Jarek 10cl, 20br, 21bl; Jocrebbin 118bl; Johnnydevil 11br; Krontus 112c; Lachris77 2tr, 42–3; Lejoch 17tl, 46t; Ron Lima 4b; Lornet 10bl; Lucidwaters 37tr; Mapics 10–11b; Milosk50 39tl; minnystock 2tl, 8–9; Evgeniya Moroz 12–13; NatashaBreen 36–7; Nikonaft 123br; Andrey Omelyanchuk 13clb; Carlos Sanchez Pereyra 118crb; Phant 4cla; Valeriya Potapova 94–5; Tom Ricciardi 48cl; Rndmst 45tr; Sandyprints 77tr; Sborisov 24bl, 28–9; Jozef Sedmak 83bl, 99tl, 105clb; Sindorei 109cra; Paula Stanley 74tl; Stevanzz 3tr, 7cl, 16c, 35b, 136–7; Stokkete 101c; Christophe Testi 98ca; Rachel Thomas 112tr; Giovanni Tiggiani 27cla; Niko Vukelic 3tl, 78–9; Tosca Weijers 130c; Shawn Williams 130br; Oleg Znamenskiyy 90bl, 96tl, 117cra.
Enoiteca Mascareta: 113cr.
Enoteca Do Colonne: 70br.
Fondazione Musei Civici di Venezia: Ca' Pesaro – Galleria Internazionale d'Arte Moderna «November» 1870 by Telemaco Signorini 57bl; Ca' Rezzonico – Museo del Settecento Veneziano Scalone d'onore, (1753–1756) by Giorgio Massari 24br; Museo Correr 57cla, Mark Edward Smith 22ca, statue of Orfeo (1775–1776) Pietra di Vicenza by Antonio Canova photo Mark Edward Smith 22ca; Museo Storico Navale 57cr; Museo del Vetro, Murano Murano Glass, Compagnia Venezia Murano, 1878 56bc; Palazzo Ducale 16bl; Palazzo Fortuny/Courtesy Galleria Traghetto Venezia Shadows by Anne-Karin Furunes photo by Mark Edward Smith 83cla.
Fondazione Teatro La Fenice: Mlchele Crosera 64tl, 64bl, 81br.
Gems of Venice: 92br.
Getty Images: Awakening 65clb; DEA/Dagli Orti 52bc, /F. Ferruzzi 11tl; DeAgostini 30–31, 33cr, 36cl;

Fine Art Images /Heritage Images 30clb; German Select / Gisela Schober 68t; Picture Pos /Kurt Hutton 53cla; Mats Silvan 25tl.
Harry's Dolci: 127cra.
iStockphoto.com: Marcus Lindstrom 12cl.
L'Isola – Carlo Moretti: 84cla.
La Caravella: 87crb.
Luigi Bevilacqua: 72bl.
Madera: 100cr.
Palazzo Mocenigo: 90cra.
Muro Venezia S. Stae: 93tr.
Museo della Musica: 74br.
Museo di Storia Naturale: 62bc.
Palazzo Grassi S.p.A : Thomas Mayer 98br.
Pamela Santini : 59cr.
Peggy Guggenheim Collection: 40–41; Attirement of the Bride 1940 by Max Ernst © ADAGP, Paris and DACS, London 2016 40bl; Donna che cammina (Femme qui marche) (1936) © The Estate of Alberto Giacometti (Fondation Giacometti, Paris and ADAGP, Paris), licensed in the UK by ACS and DACS, London 2016 41tr.
Da Rioba: 107cra.
Ristorante Linea d'Ombre: 101br.
Robert Harding Picture Library: age fotostock Doug Scott 77b; Dr. Wilfried Bahnmuller 20cl; Peter Barritt 24cla; Neil Emmerson 4cra, 21tl; Lee Frost 4clb; Sabine Lubenow 11cra, 34cla; Harrison Neil 21crb; Massimo Pizzotti 11tr; Roy Rainford 4cl; Tetra Images 4crb, 18c; Guy Thouvenin 11crb.
Studio Codex Venetia: 106tr.
Tragicomica: 92cl.
Trattoria Alla Maddalena: 121cra.
Venetia Studium: 85tc.
Venturini Souvenirs: 126crb.

Cover

Front and spine – **AWL Images:** ClickAlps .
Back – **AWL Images:** ClickAlps b; **Dreamstime. com:** Donyanedomam crb, Emicristea tr, Luca Santilli tl, Stevanzz cla.

Pull Out Map Cover

AWL Images: ClickAlps

All other images are: © Dorling Kindersley. For further information see www.dkimages.com.

Illustrator Chris Orr & Associates First edition created by Book Creation Services Ltd, London
Commissioned Photography Demetrio Carrasco, John Heseltine, Anna Mockford, Roger Moss, William Reavell, Rough Guides/Michelle Grant, Rough Guides/James McConnachie, Rough Guides/Martin Richardson

Penguin
Random
House

First Edition 2002
Published in Great Britain by
Dorling Kindersley Limited
DK, One Embassy Gardens, 8 Viaduct Gardens, London, SW11 7BW, UK
The authorised representative in the EEA is Dorling Kindersley Verlag GmbH. Arnulfstr. 124, 80636 Munich, Germany
Published in the United States by
DK Publishing, 1745 Broadway, 20th Floor, New York, NY 10019, USA
Copyright © 2002, 2023
DorlingKindersley Limited
A Penguin Random House Company
23 24 25, 26,10 9 8 7 6 5 4 3 2 1

A CIP catalogue record is available from the British Library.
A catalogue record for this book is available from the Library of Congress.

ISSN 1479-344X
ISBN 978-0-2416-2127-1
Printed and bound in Malaysia
www.dk.com

*As a guide to abbreviations in visitor information blocks: **Adm** = admission charge.*

MIX
Paper | Supporting responsible forestry
FSC™ C018179

This book was made with Forest Stewardship Council™ certified paper – one small step in DK's commitment to a sustainable future.
For more information go to www.dk.com/our-green-pledge

Phrase Book

In an Emergency

Help!	Aiuto!	eye-yoo-toh
Stop!	Fermate!	fair-mah-teh
Call a doctor.	Chiama un medico	kee-ah-mah oon meh-dee-koh
Call an ambulance.	Chiama un' ambulanza	kee-ah-mah oon am-boo-lan-tsa
Call the police.	Chiama la polizia	kee-ah-mah lah pol-ee-tsee-ah
Call the fire brigade.	Chiama i pompieri	kee-ah-mah ee pom-pee-air-ee

Communication Essentials

Yes/No	Sì/No	see/noh
Please	Per favore	pair fah-vor-eh
Thank you	Grazie	grah-tsee-eh
Excuse me	Mi scusi	mee skoo-zee
Hello	Buon giorno	bwon jor-noh
Goodbye	Arrivederci	ah-ree-veh-dair-chee
Good evening	Buona sera	bwon-ah sair-ah
What?	Quale?	kwah-leh?
When?	Quando?	kwan-doh?
Why?	Perchè?	pair-keh?
Where?	Dove?	doh-veh?

Useful Phrases

How are you?	Come sta?	koh-meh stah?
Very well, thank you.	Molto bene, grazie.	moll-toh beh-neh grah-tsee-eh
Pleased to meet you.	Piacere di conoscerla.	pee-ah-chair-eh dee-con-oh-shair-lah
That's fine.	Va bene.	va beh-neh
Where is/are …?	Dov'è/ Dove sono …?	dov-eh/doveh soh-noh …?
How do I get to …?	Come faccio per arrivare a …?	koh-meh fah choh pair arri-var-eh ah …?
Do you speak English?	Parla inglese?	par-lah een-gleh-zeh?
I don't understand.	Non capisco.	non ka-pee-skoh
I'm sorry.	Mi dispiace.	mee dee-spee-ah-cheh

Shopping

How much does this cost?	Quant'è, per favore?	kwan-teh pair fah-vor-eh?
I would like …	Vorrei …	vor-ray
Do you have …?	Avete …?	ah-veh-teh …?
Do you take credit cards?	Accettate carte di credito?	ah-chet-tah-teh kar-teh dee creh-dee-toh?
What time do you open/ close?	A che ora apre/ chiude?	ah keh or-ah ah-preh/ kee-oo-deh?
this one	questo	kweh-stoh
that one	quello	kwell-oh
expensive	caro	kar-oh
cheap	a buon prezzo	ah bwon pret-soh
size, clothes	la taglia	lah tah-lee-ah
size, shoes	il numero	eel noo-mair-oh
white	bianco	bee-ang-koh
black	nero	neh-roh
red	rosso	ross-oh
yellow	giallo	jal-loh
green	verde	vair-deh
blue	blu	bloo

Types of Shop

bakery	il forno /il panificio	eel forn-oh /eel pan-ee-fee-choh
bank	la banca	lah bang-kah
bookshop	la libreria	lah lee-breh-ree-ah
cake shop	la pasticceria	lah pas-tee-chair-ee-ah
chemist	la farmacia	lah far-mah-chee-ah
delicatessen	la salumeria	lah sah-loo-meh-ree-ah
department store	il grande magazzino	eel gran-deh mag-gad-zee-noh
grocery	la drogheria	lah droh-geh-ree-ah
hairdresser	il parrucchiere	eel par-oo-kee-air-eh
ice cream parlour	la gelateria	lah jel-lah-tair ree-ah
market	il mercato	eel mar-kah-toh
newsstand	l'edicola	leh-dee-koh-lah
post office	l'ufficio postale	loo-fee-choh pos-tah-leh
supermarket	il supermercato	eel su-pair-mair-kah-toh
tobacconist	il tabaccaio	eel tah-bak-eye-oh
travel agency	l'agenzia di viaggi	lah-jen-tsee-ah dee vee-ad-jee

Sightseeing

art gallery	la pinacoteca	lah peena-koh-teh-kah
bus stop	la fermata dell'autobus	lah fair-mah-tah dell ow-toh-booss
church	la chiesa/ la basilica	lah kee-eh-zah lah ah-seel-i-kah
closed for holidays	chiuso per le ferie	kee-oo-zoh pair leh fair-ee-eh
garden	il giardino	eel jar-dee-no
museum	il museo	eel moo-zeh-oh
railway station	la stazione	lah stah-tsee-oh-neh
tourist information	l'ufficio di turismo	loo-fee-choh dee too-ree-smoh

Staying in a Hotel

Do you have any vacant rooms?	Avete camere libere?	ah-veh-teh kah-mair-eh lee bair-eh?
double room	una camera doppia	oona kah-mair-ah doh-pee-ah
with double bed	con letto matrimoniale	kon let-toh mah-tree-moh-nee-ah-leh
twin room	una camera con due letti	oona kah-mair ah kon doo-eh let-tee
single room	una camera singola	oona kah-mair-ah sing-goh-lah
room with a bath, shower	una camera con bagno, con doccia	oona kah-mair ah kon ban-yoh, kon dot-chah
I have a reservation.	Ho fatto una prenotazione.	oh fat-toh oona preh-noh-tah-tsee-oh-neh

Eating Out

Have you got a table for …?	**Avete un tavolo per …?**	*ah-veh-teh oona tah-voh-loh pair …?*
I'd like to reserve a table.	**Vorrei prenotare un tavolo.**	*vor-ray preh-noh-tar-reh oona tah-voh-loh*
breakfast	**colazione**	*koh-lah-tsee-oh-neh*
lunch	**pranzo**	*pran-tsoh*
dinner	**cena**	*cheh-nah*
the bill	**il conto**	*eel kon-toh*
waitress	**cameriera**	*kah-mair-ee-air-ah*
waiter	**cameriere**	*kah-mair-ee-air-eh*
fixed price menu	**il menù a prezzo fisso**	*eel meh-noo ah pret-soh fee-soh*
dish of the day	**piatto del giorno**	*pee-ah-toh dell jor-no*
starter	**antipasto**	*an-tee-pass-toh*
first course	**il primo**	*eel pree-moh*
main course	**il secondo**	*eel seh-kon-doh*
vegetables	**i contorni**	*ee kon-tor-noh*
dessert	**il dolce**	*eel doll-cheh*
cover charge	**il coperto**	*eel koh-pair-toh*
wine list	**la lista dei vini**	*lah lee-stah day vee-nee*
glass	**il bicchiere**	*eel bee-kee-air-eh*
bottle	**la bottiglia**	*lah bot-teel-yah*
knife	**il coltello**	*eel kol-tell-oh*
fork	**la forchetta**	*lah for-ket-tah*
spoon	**il cucchiaio**	*eel koo-kee-eye-oh*

Menu Decoder

l'acqua minerale	*lah-kwah mee-nair- ah-leh*	mineral water
gassata/ naturale	*gah-zah-tah/ nah-too-rah-leh*	fizzy/ still
agnello	*ah-niell-oh*	lamb
aglio	*al-ee-oh*	garlic
al forno	*al for-noh*	baked
alla griglia	*ah-lah greel-yah*	grilled
la birra	*lah beer-rah*	beer
la bistecca	*lah bee-stek-kah*	steak
il burro	*eel boor-oh*	butter
il caffè	*eel kah-feh*	coffee
la carne	*la kar-neh*	meat
carne di maiale	*kar-neh dee mah-yah-leh*	pork
la cipolla	*la chip-oh-lah*	onion
i fagioli	*ee fah-joh-lee*	beans
il formaggio	*eel for-mad-joh*	cheese
le fragole	*leh frah-goh-leh*	strawberries
il fritto misto	*eel free-toh mees-toh*	mixed fried fish
la frutta	*la froot-tah*	fruit
i frutti di mare	*ee froo-tee dee mah-reh*	seafood
i funghi	*ee foon-ghee*	mushrooms
i gamberi	*ee gam-bair-ee*	prawns
il gelato	*eel jel-lah-toh*	ice cream
l'insalata	*leen-sah-lah-tah*	salad
il latte	*eel laht-teh*	milk
il manzo	*eel man-tsoh*	beef
l'olio	*loh-lee-oh*	oil
il pane	*eel pah-neh*	bread
le patate	*leh pah-tah-teh*	potatoes
le patatine fritte	*leh pah-tah-teen-eh free-teh*	chips
il pepe	*eel peh-peh*	pepper
il pesce	*eel pesh-eh*	fish
il pollo	*eel poll-oh*	chicken
il pomodoro	*eel poh-moh-dor-oh*	tomato
il prosciutto cotto/crudo	*eel pro-shoo-toh kot-toh/ kroo-doh*	ham cooked/cured
il riso	*eel ree-zoh*	rice
il sale	*eel sah-leh*	salt
la salsiccia	*lah sal-see-chah*	sausage
succo d'arancia/ di limone	*soo-koh dah-ran-chah/ dee leh-moh-neh*	orange/lemon juice
il tè	*eel teh*	tea
la torta	*lah tor-tah*	cake/tart
l'uovo	*loo-oh-voh*	egg
vino bianco	*vee-noh bee-ang-koh*	white wine
vino rosso	*vee-noh ross-oh*	red wine
le vongole	*leh von-goh-leh*	clams
lo zucchero	*loh zoo-kair-oh*	sugar
la zuppa	*lah tsoo-pah*	soup

Numbers

1	**uno**	*oo-noh*
2	**due**	*doo-eh*
3	**tre**	*treh*
4	**quattro**	*kwat-roh*
5	**cinque**	*ching-kweh*
6	**sei**	*say-ee*
7	**sette**	*set-teh*
8	**otto**	*ot-toh*
9	**nove**	*noh-veh*
10	**dieci**	*dee-eh-chee*
11	**undici**	*oon-dee-chee*
12	**dodici**	*doh-dee-chee*
13	**tredici**	*tray-dee-chee*
14	**quattordici**	*kwat-tor-dee-chee*
15	**quindici**	*kwin-dee-chee*
16	**sedici**	*say-dee-chee*
17	**diciassette**	*dee-chah-set-teh*
18	**diciotto**	*dee-chot-toh*
19	**diciannove**	*dee-chah-noh-veh*
20	**venti**	*ven-tee*
30	**trenta**	*tren-tah*
40	**quaranta**	*kwah-ran-tah*
50	**cinquanta**	*ching-kwan-tah*
60	**sessanta**	*sess-an-tah*
70	**settanta**	*set-tan-tah*
80	**ottanta**	*ot-tan-tah*
90	**novanta**	*noh-van-tah*
100	**cento**	*chen-toh*
1,000	**mille**	*mee-leh*
2,000	**duemila**	*doo-eh mee-lah*
1,000,000	**un milione**	*oon meel-yoh-neh*

Time

one minute	**un minuto**	*oon mee-noo-toh*
one hour	**un'ora**	*oon or-ah*
a day	**un giorno**	*oon jor-noh*
Monday	**lunedì**	*loo-neh-dee*
Tuesday	**martedì**	*mar-teh-dee*
Wednesday	**mercoledì**	*mair-koh-leh-dee*
Thursday	**giovedì**	*joh-veh-dee*
Friday	**venerdì**	*ven-air-dee*
Saturday	**sabato**	*sah-bah-toh*
Sunday	**domenica**	*doh-meh-nee-kah*

Selected Street Index